IMAGES
of America

The Battleship *Texas*

The Battleship *Texas* has been in the care of the Texas Parks and Wildlife Department since 1983. Its dedicated staff of professionals brought the ship back from the brink of disintegration and led her maintenance and restoration for over 30 years, a charge they tend with pride. (TPWD.)

On the Cover: The crew of *Texas* occupies every inch of horizontal surface on the front of the battleship to watch a USO show aboard ship during World War II. Here, a sailor from the crew is made part of the show. (NARA.)

IMAGES
of America

THE BATTLESHIP *TEXAS*

Mark Lardas

ARCADIA
PUBLISHING

ISBN 978-1-4671-2393-8

Published by Arcadia Publishing
Charleston, South Carolina

Printed in the United States of America

Library of Congress Control Number: 2016935276

For all general information, please contact Arcadia Publishing:
Telephone 843-853-2070
Fax 843-853-0044
E-mail sales@arcadiapublishing.com
For customer service and orders:
Toll-Free 1-888-313-2665

Visit us on the Internet at www.arcadiapublishing.com

To my three sons, Nicholas, William, and Benjamin, all of whom have spent time with me aboard Texas.

Contents

Acknowledgments

No book is the product of a single author. Many folks helped me as I wrote and assembled this book. Those I especially would like to note include my son William Lardas for accompanying me on many of my trips and doing the photography; Andy Smith, superintendent, and Stephanie Croatt, curator of the Battleship Texas State Park, for providing access to *Texas* and its archives most battleship fans can only dream about; Philip Chumlea, a model-making friend who provided many of the pictures of the refit; and Gerald Miller for use of his centennial photographs.

I would also like to thank Mike Kinsella and Matt Todd, my editors at Arcadia Publishing, for their assistance.

As well, I thank my wife, Janet, for her support during this project.

The following abbreviations indicate the sources of the illustrations used in this volume:

AC	Author's collection of images
GM	Photograph by Gerald Miller
LOC	Library of Congress
NARA	National Archives
TPWD	Texas Parks and Wildlife Department
UHDL	University of Houston Digital Archive Library
USNHHC	US Navy Naval Heritage and History Command
WL	Photograph by William Lardas

Introduction

Our story starts on April 17, 1911, when workers at Newport News Shipbuilding and Dry Dock Company laid down steel plates to form the keel of Hull No. 147. The ship was christened *Texas* at launch on May 18, 1912. When construction finished in November 1913, *Texas* was the most powerful warship in the US Navy. At 573 feet long, 95 feet, 3 inches wide, and drawing 29 feet, 7 inches when fully loaded, *Texas* displaced 27,000 tons. On builder's trials, she reached 21.79 knots.

Texas was not just a battleship. *Texas* was a dreadnought battleship. Dreadnoughts replaced the intermediate secondary battery of old-style battleships with additional main guns. Dreadnoughts had over twice the broadside of pre-dreadnought battleships.

Texas was a ship of firsts and lasts. The ninth dreadnought entering service in the US Navy when commissioned on April 12, 1914, she was the first with a main battery of 14-inch guns. *Texas* mounted 10 in five two-gun turrets, along with 21 five-inch guns and four 21-inch torpedo tubes. She was the first second-generation dreadnought (or super-dreadnought) built for the US Navy.

Texas was the last US dreadnought design built with armor of varying thickness, and the last design with reciprocating steam engines, direct drive between the engine and propellers, and coal-fired boilers. Subsequent US battleships used oil-fired boilers, which fed geared steam turbines and all-or-nothing armor.

After commissioning, *Texas* skipped the traditional shakedown cruise in response to the Tampico Incident. What started as a minor diplomatic imbroglio was enlarged by Pres. Woodrow Wilson into an American occupation of the Mexican port of Veracruz. *Texas* reinforced the US Navy fleet off Veracruz, spending an extended spring break off Mexico, remaining from May 26 through December 20, 1914.

Meanwhile, a war in Europe grew into the First World War. The United States remained neutral until April 1916, a period that *Texas* spent in routine fleet operations, training, and maintenance. Almost routine. On a foggy May 27, 1915, the Holland-American liner *Ryndam* was rammed by the fruit steamship *Joseph J. Cuneo* off the Nantucket lightship. *Texas,* with other US battleships, aided the stricken ship.

After the United States entered World War I, *Texas* was one of six US battleships sent to Europe. *Texas* joined the Royal Navy's Grand Fleet in Scotland because she burned coal. Later US battleships burned oil. Britain was short of fuel oil but had plenty of coal. *Texas* joined the war effort late; she ran aground leaving America, requiring repair. She finally arrived on February 11, 1918.

Texas saw action, but not combat. She escorted convoys across the North Sea from Britain to Norway. *Texas* only got one crack at the German High Seas Fleet, on April 25, 1918. When the High Seas Fleet steamed into the Grand Fleet, *Texas* was part of the leading battleship division. The outnumbered Germans turned and scampered back to port before anyone got in range. *Texas* next sighted the High Seas Fleet in November 1918, when the Germans sailed into Scapa Flow to surrender.

Texas returned to the United States, arriving Christmas Day 1918, and went back to peacetime service. On March 9, 1919, a Sopwith Camel took off from a platform atop *Texas*'s No. 2 turret, making *Texas* the first US battleship to launch an aircraft. Starting in 1920, *Texas* served with the Pacific Fleet, returning to the Atlantic in 1924.

Had things gone as the Navy planned, *Texas* would have been replaced by the new *Washington*-class battleship then under construction. Instead, new construction was halted due to the 1922 Naval Limitations Treaty, and *Texas* was retained and modernized.

Texas emerged from modernization in 1926 dramatically different. Gone were her distinctive cage masts, replaced by new tripod masts. Her torpedo tubes were removed. Coal-fired boilers and coal bunkers departed, replaced by more efficient oil-fired boilers and fuel-oil tanks. Six oil-fired boilers did the work of 14 coal-burning boilers. Oil fuel reduced fuel storage space. Unneeded space previously used for coal bunkers was converted to crew quarters. *Texas* gained an updated fire control system, a suite of three-inch antiaircraft guns, and an aircraft catapult.

Now the most modern battleship in the US Navy, *Texas* spent 1928 as the flagship of the United States Fleet, a role it reprised several times over the next decade. It was a decade *Texas* spent seeing duty in both the Atlantic and Pacific, transporting VIPs and showing the flag.

In 1939, World War II started. *Texas*, then the third-oldest battleship in the Navy, played an active role. In May 1941, *Texas* became part of the North Atlantic Neutrality Patrol designed to keep the war away from the Americas, escorting convoys in the Western Atlantic.

Once the United States entered World War II, *Texas* spent the first two years in the Atlantic on convoy duty. It also provided gunnery support during Operation Torch, the Anglo-American landings in western Africa. A refit in 1942 strengthened its antiaircraft battery and added radar.

In April 1944, *Texas* was assigned to support that year's scheduled invasions of France. On June 6, *Texas* participated in D-Day, bombarding German batteries at Point du Hoc, supporting the Ranger assault. Three weeks later, on June 25, at Cherbourg, *Texas* came under fire and was struck by two large shells. One was a dud, but the other exploded in the conning tower, killing the helmsman. After patching up the damage, *Texas* was off to the Mediterranean. In August, her batteries supported Operation Dragoon, Allied landings in southern France.

Texas finished 1944 with a final refit, permanently repairing battle damage and replacing the main guns. Then she was off to the Pacific. Her artillery supported landings at Iwo Jima and Okinawa, while her antiaircraft batteries fought off kamikazes. Always lucky, *Texas* escaped casualties and battle damage.

After the war, *Texas* participated in Operation Magic Carpet, transporting GIs from the Pacific to California, making two round-trips. Then she sailed to Norfolk, Virginia, and in June 1946 was placed in reserve for the first time.

Texas could have been scrapped, like the USS *Wyoming*, or expended as a target in an atom bomb test, like sister ship *New York*. Instead, *Texas* began a second life as a museum ship.

Lloyd Gregory, then general manager of the *Houston Post*, wanted *Texas* as a memorial for the state's war dead. He led a campaign to save the ship. The fact that the chief of naval operations was Chester Nimitz, a Texas native, helped. On December 6, 1946, Texas governor Coke Stevenson accepted *Texas* from the Navy.

Texas was at Baltimore. The Navy told the state it first needed to pay to move *Texas* to her proposed berth at the San Jacinto Battlefield. The state created the Battleship Texas Commission, named Lloyd Gregory as its chairman, and put the commission in charge of raising the funds to move and maintain *Texas*.

Gregory led a fundraising drive that raised money for the move, and prepared a permanent berth for *Texas*. A chunk of the cash came from contributions from Texas schoolchildren. On April 21, 1948, *Texas* arrived at her new berth at the San Jacinto Battlefield. Native son Chester Nimitz presided over a ceremony in which the Navy handed control of *Texas* to the State of Texas.

The story should end "happily ever after" here, with *Texas* spending its retirement as a monument and museum. Instead, it goes on for another 70 years. What follows is as fascinating as what went before.

Texas was built for a short life; the Navy never planned keeping her more than 20 years. Museum ships do not face the hazards of the sea or combat, but still fight time. At first all went well. The Texas Battleship Commission proved equal to running *Texas* as a public display. They found an excellent superintendent in John McKeown. A Navy veteran who had served on *Texas*, he wished nothing more than to spend the rest of his life looking after her.

The public came. Boy, did they come. By early 1952, *Texas* logged her millionth visitor. Initially, virtually every part of *Texas* was open to the general public, with much left lying around loose. Visitors took anything not secured, and some parts that were. Historic artifacts vanished.

Funding proved inadequate. *Texas* was supposed to be self-sustaining. Receipts collected were enough to pay the staff and keep *Texas* ship-shape, but not for long-term maintenance. Navy warship *Texas* had an annual dockyard overhaul. Museum ship *Texas* did not. Initially, no one realized its importance; the ship was not going anywhere.

The banks of *Texas*'s berth began eroding. Steel bulkheads were installed in 1957. In 1961, Hurricane Carla blew the radar antenna off *Texas*. By the mid-1960s, her wooden decking had rotted. It was replaced with concrete, which promised low-maintenance, waterproof protection for *Texas*'s decks. Instead, the concrete accelerated deterioration. It leaked, trapping water next to the metal, and was so heavy it buckled bulkheads.

This mistake and inadequate preventative maintenance were not the result of parsimony. Rather, the Battleship Texas Commission was in unexplored territory. *Texas* was the first battleship to be preserved. Support groups, such as the Historic Naval Ships Association, were nonexistent until 1966 when Lloyd Gregory helped create it.

Things got worse in the 1970s. McKeown died of cancer in February 1970. His replacement was not up to the job and was terminated within two years. *Texas*'s next "captain," A.G. "Spike" Taylor, a retired Coast Guard commander, began setting things right—just in time. Complaints about *Texas*'s condition led to a Navy inspection in November 1971. *Texas* passed largely due to Taylor's work.

Texas touched bottom over the next 15 years—literally. Ill health led Lloyd Gregory to resign from the commission in 1974. The Battleship Texas Commission and staff experienced high turnover. A bureaucratic turf war between the Battleship Texas Commission and Texas Parks and Wildlife Department (TPWD) over control of *Texas* consumed energy better spent fixing the battleship. Conditions aboard *Texas*, including problems from deteriorating fuel oil still aboard since 1948, created an unhealthy environment.

In 1983, the state government abolished the Battleship Texas Commission, putting the warship under TPWD jurisdiction. Three groups of volunteers formed to help restore *Texas* in 1985 and merged into the First Texas Volunteers in 1986.

In 1986, *Texas* sank at her moorings due to underwater leaks. While patched and refloated, it was obvious volunteer efforts could not save *Texas*. Over the next year, a major fundraising campaign and the state government raised money to repair *Texas*. In 1988, *Texas* was towed to Todd Shipyard in Galveston, dry docked, and repaired. The hull was patched, and the ship restored to its 1945 appearance, down to the paint job.

Texas returned in 1990 in better shape than she had been since her 1944 refit. Since then, *Texas* has been in the competent hands of TPWD staff, although parts of *Texas* have been restored by volunteers. She celebrated the 100th anniversary of her launch in 2012.

Challenges remain. The engine rooms were closed from 2007 through 2010 for restoration. New leaks occurred in 2012. While patching those leaks, it was discovered that the hull below the engines was about to collapse. Repairs, done in place, took two years.

As for the future of *Texas*? The staff of the Battleship *Texas* takes the long view, aiming to preserve the ship for another century. This includes placing *Texas* in a dry berth to reduce corrosion. With work and luck, the ship will celebrate a bicentennial at the San Jacinto battlefield.

Pictured is the Battleship *Texas* today, restored to her 1945 configuration in her berth at the San Jacinto Battleground Park. (WL.)

One

NAVY WARSHIP

Texas spent her first 36 years as a vessel of the US Navy. Construction, from keel-laying to commissioning, took two years, and she spent her final two years in the Navy laid up, "awaiting disposal." In between, from 1914 to 1946, she was a commissioned warship, a dreadnought battleship. She was the most powerful warship in the world when commissioned. Even at the end of her career, she could still outpunch almost any other US surface warship, except the 24 other dreadnought battleships then in commission with the Navy.

Texas saw a lot of action during those three dozen years. She took part in the Veracruz intervention shortly after being commissioned in 1914. During World War I, *Texas* was one of only six Navy dreadnoughts to operate with the Grand Fleet out of Scapa Flow. She almost got a shot at the German High Seas Fleet in April 1918, but German admiral Reinhard Scheer took his ships home when he spotted the American ships coming.

Not until World War II did *Texas* actually see combat. By then, it was one of the oldest ships in the fleet. Despite its age, it served throughout the war. Even before the United States entered World War II, *Texas* was part of America's North Atlantic Neutrality Patrol. After US entry into the war, *Texas* provided gunnery support for the North African landings, the Normandy invasion, and the invasion of southern France. In 1945, *Texas* served in the Pacific, fighting at Iwo Jima and Okinawa. Remarkably, the only combat casualties she suffered in four years of fighting were in June 1944. While bombarding Cherbourg, *Texas* was struck by two shells from a German shore battery.

During her career as a Navy warship, *Texas* was home for the 1,800 men serving aboard her. Men worked, slept, ate, and played aboard *Texas*. In many ways, *Texas* resembled a small town, complete with a barbershop, soda fountain, tailor shop, post office, and laundry. She even had her own sports teams.

This chapter presents a visual essay into *Texas* as a warship and a home.

USS *Texas* was one of two New York–class battleships authorized by Congress in 1910. She was built at the Newport News Shipbuilding and Dry Dock Company's shipyard in Newport News, Virginia. This image shows the building ways shortly after the keel of *Texas* was laid down on April 17, 1911. (TPWD.)

Construction advanced quickly. By July 1, 1911, seventy-four days after the keel had been framed, the bulkheads in the machinery areas of *Texas* were in place. Yet the hull was far from being completed. Work on the armored citadel had not yet begun. (TPWD.)

It took 13 months to complete construction of *Texas*'s hull. This picture shows the hull, ready for launching in May 1912. (LOC.)

The launching of any major US Navy warship was considered an important event, and *Texas*'s launching was celebrated with great fanfare and ceremony. Here, a crowd made up of dignitaries, dockyard workers, and the curious public gathers in advance of the spectacle. (LOC.)

By 1912, Navy custom called for a launched ship to be sponsored by someone, usually a young woman, christening it with a bottle of something. *Texas* was launched during the administration of William Howard Taft. As a result, *Texas*'s sponsor was Claudia Lyon, the daughter of Col. Cecil Lyon, Republican national committeeman from Texas. The young lady, pictured in the dress she wore at the christening, appears unimpressed with the honor, sporting the "I'm bored," expression still used by girls in their early teens today. (LOC.)

Launches were preceded by speeches and a public blessing of the ship. *Texas* was one of only two US battleships launched in 1912. Present at the launching of the *Texas* was Secretary of the Navy George von Lengerke Meyer, who can be seen standing next to Claudia Lyon. (LOC.)

Claudia Lyon, holding a bouquet of flowers and a bottle of champagne, prepares to christen *Texas* by breaking the bottle against her bow. Having a young girl handle a bottle of alcohol caused an uproar among the many citizens of Texas, especially Prohibition-minded progressive elements in the state. (LOC.)

On May 18, 1912, *Texas* slid down the launch ways into the waters of Chesapeake Bay. Her hull touched saltwater for the first time, accompanied by the cheers of the crowd. Aboard were some of the shipyard workers who built the ship, feeling the accomplishment of their completed work. (LOC.)

Texas, floating free for the first time, is pictured shortly after her launching. A tug steams towards it to take *Texas* in tow. The hull is riding high in the water, with a lot of the lower hull visible. Fully loaded, the waterline would be close to the top of the lighter color. (LOC.)

Texas was far from complete when launched. Still to be added were her engines, her boilers, her armament, and much of her armor. It would take another 15 months' worth of work before *Texas* was ready for acceptance trials. (TPWD.)

In October 1913, *Texas* underwent speed runs to test her propulsion system and handling. This picture was taken during the 24th run, on October 27. It achieved a speed of 21.79 knots, above her design speed of 21 knots. *Texas* is not yet complete, though. Note the unfinished after mast. (NARA.)

Texas was commissioned as a unit of the US Navy on March 12, 1914. She is pictured here at Norfolk Naval Yard on March 24, 1914, shortly after she was commissioned and just before her departure for New York's Brooklyn Naval Yard. (LOC.)

After her commissioning, *Texas* would have been open for visitors, as shown here. It was an opportunity to display the newest and most powerful ship in the US Navy to the general public. The gun pictured is a five-inch cannon, part of *Texas*'s secondary battery. (LOC.)

Capt. Albert W. Grant was the first captain of the *Texas*. He took the ship through her acceptance trials and remained captain until 1915, when he turned command of the battleship over to John Hood. In 1918, by then a vice admiral, Grant commanded the Atlantic Fleet. (LOC.)

Dogs served as mascots for *Texas* through much of her service in the US Navy. The tradition started early. Mamma dog was already aboard in 1914 when she gave birth to a litter of puppies. The delighted crew declared the dogs the new family of the battleship. (TPWD.)

Texas arrived in New York Harbor on March 27, 1914. It is seen here surrounded by tugs. It spent the next five weeks at the Brooklyn Naval Yard, where the ship's fire control system was installed. (LOC.)

Texas did not remain in New York. On May 13, she sailed to Veracruz, Mexico, to enforce the occupation of the customhouse following the Tampico Incident. It joined battleships *Utah* and *Florida*, as well as five destroyers and two submarines. *Texas* went to operational status without the normal shakedown cruise. (TPWD.)

Following duty at Veracruz, *Texas* used the opportunity to make her first visit to her namesake state. While at Galveston, Captain Grant accepted a silver service presented to the ship by the State of Texas. The silver service was purchased by the Young Men's Business League of Waco, which presented it for the state. (TPWD.)

Texas was soon back in New York. It may have been during that stay that it paraded at night with sister battleship *New York*, using electrical lighting to outline the ships. This remarkable picture, captured in 1915, resulted. (LOC.)

In 1915, *Texas* acquired a 1:100 scale silver model of the 17th-century Dutch admiral de Ruyter's flagship, *De Zeven Provincien*. The model was presented by the Holland-American Line after *Texas* assisted the crew and passengers of the steamer *Ryndam* following her collision with another ship off Nantucket on May 27, 1915. It remains on display aboard the ship. (LOC.)

Sailors took pride in their ship, especially when it was the newest battleship in the Navy. This picture, taken in 1914 or 1915, shows four sailors demonstrating the size of *Texas*'s 14-inch main guns, then the largest in the fleet. The barrel could accommodate a husky sailor. With a 14-inch diameter, a man with a waist of 42 inches or less could fit. Few sailors were that hefty before World War I. (TPWD.)

Texas spent 1916 on maneuvers with the fleet. That period included a stay at Guantanamo Bay, which can be seen in the background of this photograph. *New York* is behind *Texas*; a *Pennsylvania*-class battleship is to *Texas*'s right. *Texas* and *New York* sport an "E" on the after funnel for gunnery excellence. (USNHHC.)

World War I started in 1914. Later, in 1916, *Texas* returned to New York City for an overhaul. The United States was still neutral in 1916 (Wilson ran for reelection using the slogan "He kept us out of the war"), but storm clouds were gathering. (USNHHC.)

The United States wanted its Navy ready to fight. To prepare *Texas* for war, she was dry docked and her bottom cleaned and painted to improve her performance. This photograph shows *Texas* after her bottom was scraped but before she was painted. Painting stages have been rigged. (USNHHC.)

In 1916, the bottom of a ship was painted by hand, using brushes and mops. This team of sailors is painting *Texas*'s stern, over the propeller shaft. The lack of harnesses or other safety equipment is evident. (TPWD.)

Once the United States entered World War I, *Texas* was one of five battleships sent to Europe to serve with the British Grand Fleet. The rest of the squadron arrived on December 7, 1917, cheered by British sailors. *Texas* arrived on February 11, 1918, delayed by repairs after it grounded in September 1917. (USNHHC.)

Texas's captain during World War I was Victor Blue, a name that would have served a battleship captain in a boy's adventure novel. As a lieutenant during the Spanish-American War, he conducted a daring intelligence mission behind Spanish lines. He is shown aboard *Texas* after his promotion to admiral. (USNHHC.)

On August 29, 1918, while in the Firth of Forth, in Scotland, *Texas* was visited by Assistant Secretary of the Navy Franklin D. Roosevelt. He is shown here being presented to *Texas*'s officers by Capt. Victor Blue. Roosevelt later became president, the first of four American presidents to set foot on *Texas*. (NARA.)

With the war over, *Texas* returned to the United States, arriving at New York for an overhaul on Christmas Day 1918. Among the changes made during the overhaul were the removal of the forward and stern five-inch guns and the addition of a ramp on Turret 2 for aircraft. (USNHHC.)

Texas now carried a Sopwith Camel, a British fighter aircraft used by the United States. On March 19, 1919, it flew off the *Texas* while the ship was anchored in Guantanamo Bay, and *Texas* became the first American battleship to launch an aircraft. (USNHHC.)

The summer of 1919, *Texas* was reassigned to the Pacific Fleet. This required it to transit the Panama Canal, as pictured here. It was the first time it took the big ditch but was far from the last. *Texas* is in the Galliard (now Culebra) Cut, approaching Rio Chagres. (USNHHC.)

The Panama Canal has three sets of locks. *Texas*, right, and *Arkansas*, left, are seen here in the Gatun Locks on July 25, 1919, the last set of locks before they reach the Pacific Ocean. The ships are towed through the locks by electric locomotives called *mulas* (mules). (USNHHC.)

Once in the Pacific, *Texas* became part of the Navy's Pacific Fleet. *Texas* participated in the annual battle maneuvers, which involved live gunnery practice at full speed. She has just fired her main battery of 14-inch guns. (USHHC)

Texas was more than a warship. She was home to her crew. Her peacetime complement numbered 1,059 men. In World War I, the crew was over 1,400, and by World War II, it exceeded 1,800. *Texas* needed facilities to make it a home, which included a barbershop, pictured here in 1914. Yes, there is a cash register. (TPWD.)

Texas also had a dentist's office. A sailor could make an appointment for everything from a simple checkup to something as complicated as getting a filling—although between the two world wars, a dentist was more likely to pull a tooth than fill it. (TPWD.)

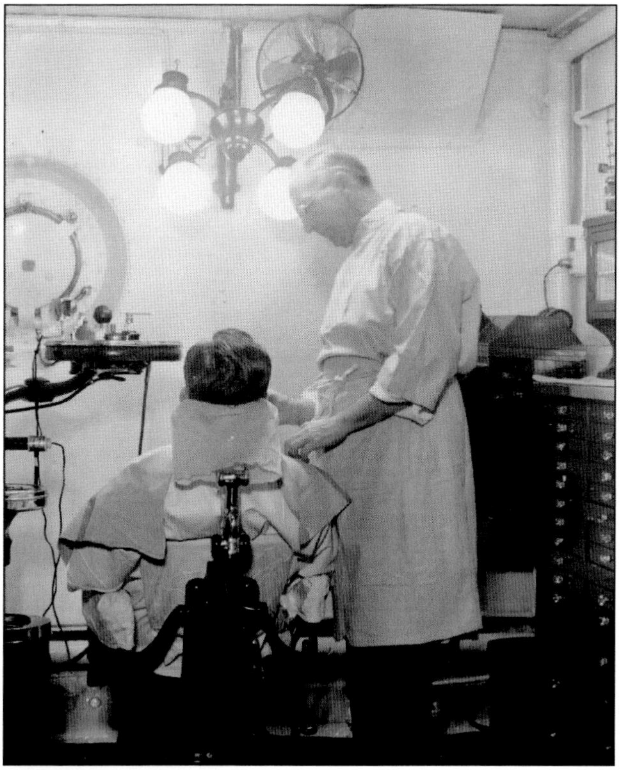

Her crew went through a lot of food. A big draw for joining the Navy was the three hot meals sailors got daily. The food was prepared in *Texas*'s galleys. The main galley, pictured here, was on the upper deck at the aft end of the superstructure. (TPWD.)

Texas's crew also went through a lot of bread daily. In the 19th century this would have been hard tack, but *Texas*, like all 20th-century US Navy battleships, had a bakery to turn out fresh loaves of bread for her men, as well as sheets of cobbler for desert. (TPWD.)

Another necessary facility aboard *Texas* was the laundry, shown here, with some of the men assigned to run it. As can be seen, the US Navy in the first half of the 20th century was not a smoke-free environment. (TPWD.)

Competitive sports played an important role for American sailors. This boxing match was held aboard *Texas* during the Battle Fleet maneuvers in 1923. The ring was set up between Turrets 3 and 4. The banner on the back of Turret 4 reads "Come On Texas," the ship's slogan. (USNHHC.)

Life aboard a battleship was more "regulation" than it was for sailors aboard smaller ships. This included meals, especially for the leaders. Pictured here is a meal in the warrant officers' mess. It is a formal meal with a full place setting, white tablecloths, and mess attendants serving the food. (NARA.)

Life aboard a battleship also meant constant loading of supplies and ammunition. The most miserable job might have been loading coal, which was heavy and dirty, but loading the shells for the 14-inch main guns came a close second. A 14-inch shell weighed up to 1,400 pounds, and hundreds had to be loaded. (TPWD.)

While mechanical hoists were used to move the shells, it still took muscle—and plenty of it—to position the shells for the trip to the magazine. Topping off the main battery was an all-hands effort. *Texas* stored the shells nose first in the magazine. (TPWD.)

Between 1919 and 1925, sister ships *New York* (left) and *Texas* (right) underwent annual overhauls, sometimes at the same time, as in this picture taken at Norfolk Navy Yard in the mid-1920s. Generally, they experienced minor modifications, such as the two forward five inch guns being removed. In 1925 and 1926, the ships went through a major overhaul. (USNHHC.)

The 1922 Naval Limitations Treaty meant keeping *Texas* 10 years longer than planned, and the battleship required modification to extend her life. The biggest change was replacing the 14 coal-fired boilers with six more powerful oil-fired boilers. These new boilers were originally built for the scrapped *Washington*-class battleships intended to replace *Texas* and *New York*. (USNHHC.)

During this modernization overhaul, the main battery of 14-inch guns *Texas* had used since 1914 was removed and replaced with new barrels. These are five of the new barrels installed during this refit. (TPWD.)

The *Texas* emerging from the overhaul was much different than her earlier configuration. She only needed one smokestack, the cage mast had been replaced by tripod masts, and the torpedo tubes were removed. Most of the lower deck five-inch guns were removed, with six relocated to the upper deck. (USNHHC.)

Torpedo blisters were installed, increasing *Texas*'s beam. The antiaircraft armament was increased to eight three-inch guns. An aircraft catapult was installed on Turret 3 amidships, so *Texas* could carry spotter aircraft. Larger cranes were installed to handle both aircraft and the ship's boats. (USNHHC.)

In 1927, following completion of the overhaul, *Texas* served as flagship for the US Navy. Shortly afterwards, in January 1928, *Texas* carried Pres. Calvin Coolidge to Havana for the Pan-American conference. She returned to duties with the Scouting Fleet in 1928. This included the gunnery practice pictured here. (USNHHC.)

Coolidge was not the only celebrity to visit *Texas* in the late 1920s. Another visitor was Charles "Lucky Lindy" Lindbergh, who visited the ship in February 1929. Of course, he was photographed in one of the aircraft carried aboard *Texas* at that time, a Vought O2U Corsair. (TPWD.)

In March 1931, Secretary of the Navy Charles Francis Adams inspected the *Texas*. He is accompanied by *Texas*'s captain, Adolphus Andrews, as sailors in their best white uniforms "toe the line," standing at attention lined up along a plank seam. Andrews was a Texas native, born in Galveston. (USNHHC.)

Between 1931 and 1937, *Texas* was assigned to the Pacific, homeported in San Diego, California, and serving as fleet flagship and First Battle Division flagship. In 1937, *Texas* was reassigned to the Atlantic, where she would remain for the next nine years. *Texas* is seen here in the Gatun Lock on June 21, 1937. (USNHHC.)

Texas is dressed with flags for Navy Day, October 27, 1940. The United States was still at peace, but World War II had been going on for over a year. *Texas* still had some lower deck casemate five-inch guns and the five-inch gun mounted above the main deck at this time. (USNHHC.)

By 1941, *Texas* was at war, even if the United States was still technically neutral. In May 1941, *Texas* began operating on the North Atlantic Neutrality Patrol, patrolling the western North Atlantic. She is seen here silhouetted against the sunset while participating in North Atlantic convoy operations in the summer of 1941. (USNHHC.)

In the summer of 1942, *Texas* went through another refit, which altered her appearance close to what she has today. The ship acquired a Measure 12 camouflage paint job, which can be most clearly seen in this side view. The remaining lower deck five-inch guns were removed and the casemates plated over. This photograph, along with the two on the next page, were taken on August 19, 1942, shortly after *Texas* finished her refit at the Norfolk Navy Yard. (TPWD.)

The refit beefed up *Texas*'s antiaircraft battery. The low-angle five-inch gun above the air castle was replaced by three-inch antiaircraft guns, raising the total to 10, and numerous light antiaircraft guns were added. Also added, visible in this bow view, was improved radar, both surface and air search. (TPWD.)

The stern view of *Texas* after her 1942 refit is shown here. By October, the newly refurbished *Texas* would be off the coast of North Africa, supporting the Torch invasions. (TPWD.)

Texas spent most of 1943 escorting convoys across the North Atlantic Ocean. It was photographed here by a patrolling aircraft while 10 miles off the Virginia coast near Norfolk on December 9, 1943. Note the numerous 20-mm and 40-mm antiaircraft guns on the deck. (USNHHC.)

Twelve days later, on December 21, 1943, *Texas* was back off Norfolk. This bow shot shows *Texas* completely covered with antiaircraft guns. *Texas* no longer had a primary mission of fighting other battleships. Rather, her role had change to providing gunnery support and antiaircraft cover during amphibious invasions. (USNHHC.)

The biggest invasion in Europe was Operation Overlord in France, on the Normandy coast, and *Texas* would play a role. The commander of Operation Overlord, Gen. Dwight D. Eisenhower, who would later become president, is pictured aboard *Texas* a few weeks before the June 1944 invasion speaking to her crew. (USNHHC.)

June 6 found *Texas* off Utah Beach, providing fire support. This picture, taken from *Texas* on the morning of the invasion, shows the bombardment of Point du Hoc, where Army Rangers would land to seize German shore batteries. HMS *Glasgow* was part of the Allied fleet on that day. (USNHHC.)

That afternoon, Lieutenant Commander Knapper and Chief Yeoman Cook from the *Texas* went ashore to examine the results of their battleship's shooting. They are pictured in a damaged German pillbox at Pointe du Hoc, captured only a few hours earlier by the 2nd Ranger Battalion, led by Texas native Col. James Rudder. (USHHC)

After the invasion, *Texas* served as a temporary prison camp for some of the German and Italian soldiers captured on D-Day. Armed guards from the US Army lead a line of prisoners aboard as *Texas* sailors watch. The prisoners sprawled on the deck are suffering from seasickness. (USNHHC.)

Texas's sick bay and surgery was used in the days after the invasion. A casualty, possibly one of the Rangers injured at Point du Hoc, is hoisted aboard *Texas* in a Stokes basket, so the ship's surgeons can treat him. Many injured Rangers were taken to *Texas*. (NARA.)

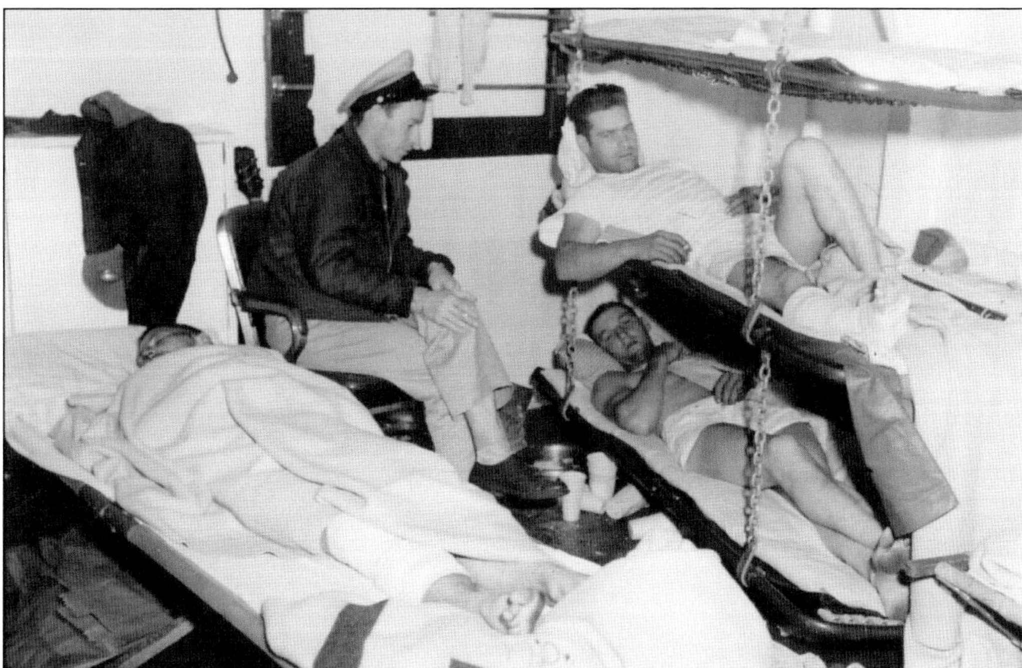

It was impractical for the wounded to remain on the beachhead. After being treated, these three soldiers, injured at Normandy on June 6, were cared for aboard *Texas* until they could be transferred to Britain. *Texas* returned to Plymouth, England, to resupply on June 8. (NARA.)

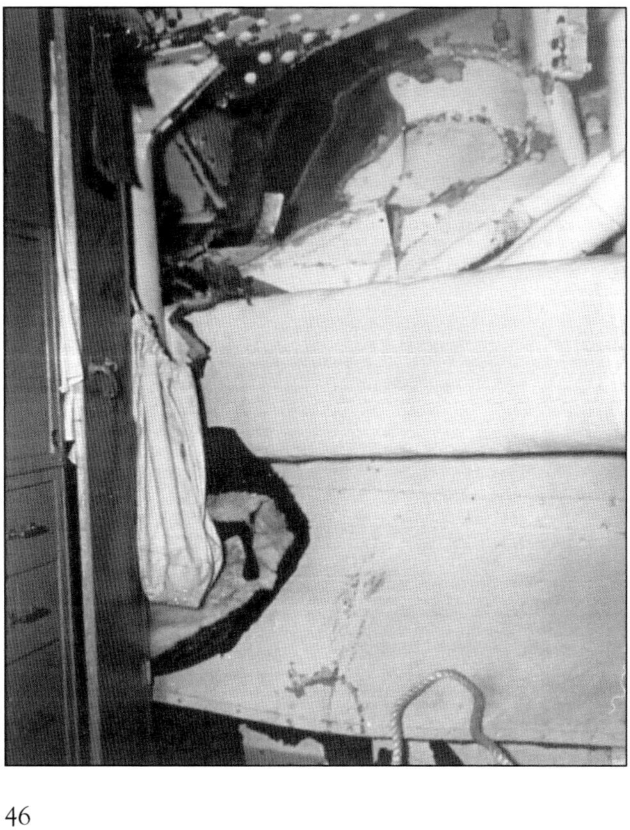

On June 25, battleships *Texas* and *Arkansas* began shelling shore batteries protecting the German-held French port of Cherbourg. The batteries fired back. This picture, taken from the *Arkansas*, shows one of the German shells landing near *Texas*. *Texas* exchanged fire with the Germans for three hours, expending 208 14-inch rounds. (USNHHC.)

The Germans straddled or near missed *Texas* 65 times but only hit twice. One hit, a 240-mm shell, struck the top of the conning tower, killing the helmsman and wounding others; *Texas*'s first combat casualties. A 240-mm shell struck forward but failed to explode. It damaged one officer's cabin, as shown here. (NARA.)

The dud shell was defused and disarmed. When *Texas* had an overhaul at the Brooklyn Naval Yard in October 1944, dockyard workers presented the restored shell to Rear Adm. Carleton F. Bryant (left) and Capt. Charles A. Baker, *Texas*'s commanding officer. It was kept as a lucky charm. (USNHHC.)

Texas spent July and August 1944 off the French Riviera. The trip was not a summer vacation; *Texas* provided gunnery support during the invasion of southern France. *Texas* bombarded a German 155-mm battery off St. Tropez and fired an additional 172 14-inch rounds to help the invading soldiers. (USNHHC.)

Texas went through a month-long refit in September and October 1944. The 14-inch gun barrels were replaced, damage repaired, and additional antiaircraft guns and new radar installed. *Texas* also got a new Measure 21 paint job: solid Navy Blue. Christmas saw *Texas* at Pearl Harbor. This picture was taken in January 1945. (USNHHC.)

There was time for play aboard *Texas* during World War II, as well as fighting. This USO show was held aboard ship, with the crew crowding the decks forward to watch. Here, a sailor from the crew is made part of the show. (NARA.)

Drones, pilotless, remote-controlled aircraft, are a big thing today, but they have a long history. While *Texas* was in Hawaiian waters in January 1945, it hosted drone tests. Here, a drone is being launched off *Texas*'s catapult on January 4, 1945. (NARA.)

Texas would support two more amphibious landings in 1945 before the war ended: Iwo Jima in February and Okinawa in April. The dud shell must have brought luck, because *Texas* was spared kamikaze damage during those battles. This is *Texas* among the landing forces off Iwo Jima. (USNHHC.)

This view shows the Iwo Jima beaches from *Texas* on February 17, 1945. Minesweepers are clearing channels for landing craft. During two days of post-landing bombardment and two weeks of fire support afterwards, *Texas* fired 923 14-inch shells. (USNHHC.)

Two

Museum Ship and Monument

Texas fought in two world wars and spent 36 years in the Navy. It has been a war memorial and a museum ship for nearly twice that length of time: 68 years by the time this book was written. It has spent most of those years peacefully sitting in a mooring near the San Jacinto Battlefield, yet it has had more near misses and close calls with destruction than it ever did as a naval warship.

Its first escape from oblivion came after World War II. The four Navy battleships closest in age to *Texas*, including sister ship *New York*, were expended as targets during atomic bomb tests. The rest were scrapped. *Texas* was spared that fate because its home state wanted it as a monument. Instead, it became a proud symbol of Texas heritage.

Despite the enthusiasm for *Texas*, those responsible for the ship lacked both the money and knowledge to really properly care for the ship. By the late 1970s, *Texas* was in poor shape, even as its historical value grew. During the 1980s, *Texas* went through an adventure as desperate as any it faced during wartime. The citizens of Texas rallied around their ship one more time, raising the funds to restore it. It proved just in the nick of time. *Texas* almost sank on its way to dry dock.

The ship emerged in better shape than it had been since its last Navy refit in 1944. But time is a relentless foe, and two decades later, *Texas* faced another battle with age, undergoing another refit, this one in place. For seven decades, *Texas* has drawn Texans, Navy veterans, and fans of historic vessels everywhere. It has had millions of visitors and been the scene of reunions and celebrations.

Believe nothing exciting or interesting happens to a museum ship? This chapter hopefully proves this belief wrong. It illustrates the experiences of the everyday visitors, the personalities who looked after *Texas*, and some of the more interesting events that have taken place on the Battleship *Texas* during its tenure in Texas.

After World War II ended, the Navy did not need the obsolete Battleship *Texas*. It would have been scrapped, but the State of Texas wanted to preserve it. The first step was finding a permanent home for the battleship, and in 1946, a slip was dredged at the San Jacinto Battlefield. (TPWD.)

Texas was laid up in Norfolk awaiting disposal when the State of Texas claimed its namesake battleship, paying the costs associated with transferring her to Houston. This included removing the propellers and propeller shafts and plating the opening. *Texas* was towed from Virginia to Texas. (TPWD.)

Three tugs pushed *Texas* into her slip in April 1948. It was still a US Navy warship, manned by a Navy crew. The official transfer to the State of Texas took place on April 21, 1948, as part of that year's San Jacinto Day celebration. Note the speaker's platform atop Turret 3. (TPWD.)

The final Navy crew of *Texas* poses for a photograph after delivering the ship to the San Jacinto Battlefield Park. Note the chief petty officer sixth from the left in the first standing row. He is MMC John "Tiger Jack" McKeown, who served aboard *Texas* during her final 13 years in the Navy. (TPWD.)

Crowds gathered at *Texas*'s new berth at the San Jacinto Battlefield to watch the arrival of the battleship. This picture was taken from the ship. (USNHHC.)

Among the speakers present on April, 21, 1948, when *Texas* was turned over to the State of Texas were Assistant Secretary of the Navy Mark Andrews (left) and Admiral of the Fleet Chester W. Nimitz (looking up). They are sitting on the speaker's platform aboard *Texas*. (USNHHC.)

Chester Nimitz, shown signing a program at the dedication ceremony, was a Texas native who grew up in Fredericksburg. During World War II, he commanded the Pacific Fleet and became one of only five six-star admirals in the US Navy. His grandfather's Nimitz Hotel in Fredericksburg is now part of the Chester Nimitz National Museum of the Pacific War. Nimitz helped Texas obtain the Battleship *Texas*. (USNHHC.)

Dignitaries board *Texas* prior to the dedication ceremony. They are met by an honor guard made up of *Texas*'s sailors saluting and Marines presenting arms. (USNHHC.)

After the ceremony was over, the public was invited aboard to tour *Texas*. It would be opening day for *Texas* as a museum ship and war memorial. To accommodate crowds, a temporary gangway was installed on the port side for departing guests. (USNHHC.)

As befits occasions involving Navy warships and naval history, the US Navy sent an active-duty warship. The Allen B. Sumner–class destroyer *Charles S. Sperry*, then a training ship operating out of New Orleans, attended the ceremonies as a representative of the Navy. (USNHHC.)

Texas was turned over to the state with most of the equipment remaining on board. This included this knot board, used to train *Texas* crewmen when the ship was in naval service. It contained examples of virtually every knot, hitch, or splice of use to a sailor. (TPWD.)

John McKeown was hired as the assistant caretaker for *Texas* after leaving the Navy in 1948. Within a year, he was the caretaker, styling himself "Captain" of *Texas*. McKeown (right) is pictured in his uniform: a chief's jacket with Navy captain's rank insignia and a white service cap with a US Army officer's national insignia. He is shaking hands with Leo West when the retired West visited the battleship; West served aboard *Texas* during both world wars. (TPWD.)

McKeown lived aboard *Texas* in the captain's quarters for over 20 years. His companions were three miniature English bulldogs, Jiggs, Pogo, and Pat. Pogo and Pat are pictured here, standing on the hood of McKeown's automobile. (TPWD.)

Another important figure in the Battleship *Texas* as a museum ship was Lloyd Gregory (right). A newspaperman, he led the drive to preserve *Texas.* He was appointed chairman of the Battleship Texas Commission, chartered by the state government to operate the site, and served on the commission for 25 years. (TPWD.)

In 1949, while flagship for Britain's West Indies Squadron, HMS *Glasgow* made a port visit to Houston. *Glasgow*, a *Towns*-class cruiser and a sister ship to the now preserved HMS *Belfast*, was a veteran of the Normandy landings, along with *Texas. Glasgow*'s crew is turned out to salute *Texas* as it passes. (TPWD.)

In 1952, Ernest Hudgens of Lufkin, Texas, was proclaimed the official one millionth visitor to the Battleship *Texas* when he came aboard with his son Ernest Hudgens Jr. and his son's friend Fred Childers (far left). Captain McKeown and Lloyd Gregory are shown congratulating Hudgens and awarding an autographed program. The son still has the program and this photograph. (TPWD.)

The Hudgenses were one of many families visiting *Texas* while it has been a monument. This picture, taken in 1949, shows a father with his young daughter on his lap sitting at one of the 20-mm mounts. He might have been a World War II veteran who served aboard *Texas*. (TPWD.)

In 1957, nine years after *Texas* became a museum ship, mom and kids from another family pose for a photograph above the galley. Presumably dad is taking the picture. *Texas* was a popular spot for a family outing in the 1950s. (TPWD.)

In a photograph dated 1966–1967, a dad and two daughters wave to the camera while next to one of the port side three-inch guns aboard *Texas*. Dad's father might have served aboard *Texas*, or it might just be an opportunity to see a surviving World War II warship. (TPWD.)

Texas is pictured at San Jacinto Battlefield Park in 1954, still in relatively good shape. At this time, most of the battleship, both interior and exterior, was accessible to the public. There have been few modifications to the ship or the mooring since 1948. (TPWD.)

Both of *Texas*'s propellers were removed when preparing her as a museum ship. One was kept aboard when it was delivered to the state. In the 1950s, that propeller was displayed on the forward starboard upper deck. (TPWD.)

By the mid-1950s, *Texas*'s slip was eroding away. To keep the shore around *Texas* from sliding into the berth, the Battleship Texas Commission had a bulkhead installed around the mooring. This shows Brown and Root putting in the bulkhead in February 1956. (TPWD.)

This iconic photograph of *Texas* was taken in 1956. A tanker steams up the Houston Ship Channel, past *Texas*, with the San Jacinto Monument in the background. *Texas*'s appearance differs from the *Texas* of 1943–1945, with much fewer 20-mm and 40-mm guns mounted. These were removed following World War II so the guns could be installed on more modern ships. (UHDL.)

Texas is pictured here in 1960. Her appearance is little changed from the day she arrived at San Jacinto Battlefield Park in 1948. Hurricane Carla, which struck Houston in 1961, wrought significant changes to *Texas*, however. Carla destroyed the radar antennas and damaged exposed areas of the old battleship. (TPWD.)

Between 1948 and 1982, the Battleship *Texas* was managed by the Battleship Texas Commission, a state commission whose members were appointed by the Texas governor. The commission often met in *Texas*'s captain's quarters. They are pictured here at her dining table. Lloyd Gregory is in the second row, third from left, and John McKeown is in the second row, far right. (TPWD.)

By 1967, *Texas*'s wooden deck was rotting. Between 1968 and 1969, the entire deck was replaced with concrete. At the time, it was believed concrete offered a light, waterproof, and low-cost alternative to wood. Instead, it trapped water below the concrete, promoting corrosion. It also proved heavier than wood, causing some bulkheads under it to buckle. (PC.)

Lloyd Gregory finally retired from the Battleship Texas Commission in 1974. He is shown here giving a farewell address on the battleship. Gregory was replaced by Rear Adm. (Retired) C.H. Taylor. By the 1970s, the condition of *Texas* was growing critical, despite Gregory's devotion to the ship. (TPWD.)

Even as *Texas* deteriorated, more groups were recognizing the historic significance of the old warship. In 1975, the American Society of Mechanical Engineers named *Texas* a National Historic Mechanical Engineering Landmark. *Texas* contained the largest surviving triple-expansion steam engines on any ship afloat. (WL.)

Another famous visitor boarded *Texas* on San Jacinto Day in 1976, then first lady Betty Ford. To her left is A.G. "Spike" Taylor, who served as captain of *Texas* from 1971 through 1978. Taylor's restoration efforts kept *Texas* from deteriorating past recovery. (TPWD.)

The bicentennial of the United States occurred in 1976, and the San Jacinto Day celebration that year was celebrated with extra ceremony and special guests, such as Betty Ford. Among other special guests were commission members. Pictured are Ralph Block (at podium), and, from right to left, Adm. Philip Koelsch, Frank Tritico, and George R. Brown. (TPWD.)

In 1976, *Texas* achieved another honor. It was named a National Historic Landmark by the National Park Service. The plaque proclaiming *Texas*'s new status is presented by T.R. Thompson of the National Park Service to the then chair of the Battleship Texas Committee, Ralph Block. (TPWD.)

By the late 1970s, when this picture was taken, *Texas* still looked good from the outside. A visitor approaching it would be impressed by her seeming permanence. In reality, *Texas* had serious problems and could not remain viable as a museum ship if those were not addressed. (TPWD.)

Inadequate maintenance left many exposed parts of *Texas* at the mercy of the elements. By 1983, when these pictures were taken, the five-inch guns on the air castle had rusted so badly they were frozen in place. (PC.)

The concrete on the decks leaked from the time it was installed in 1969. By 1983, the concrete had cracked, providing a pathway for water to seep down to the steel below. Water remained trapped and could not dry out. (PC.)

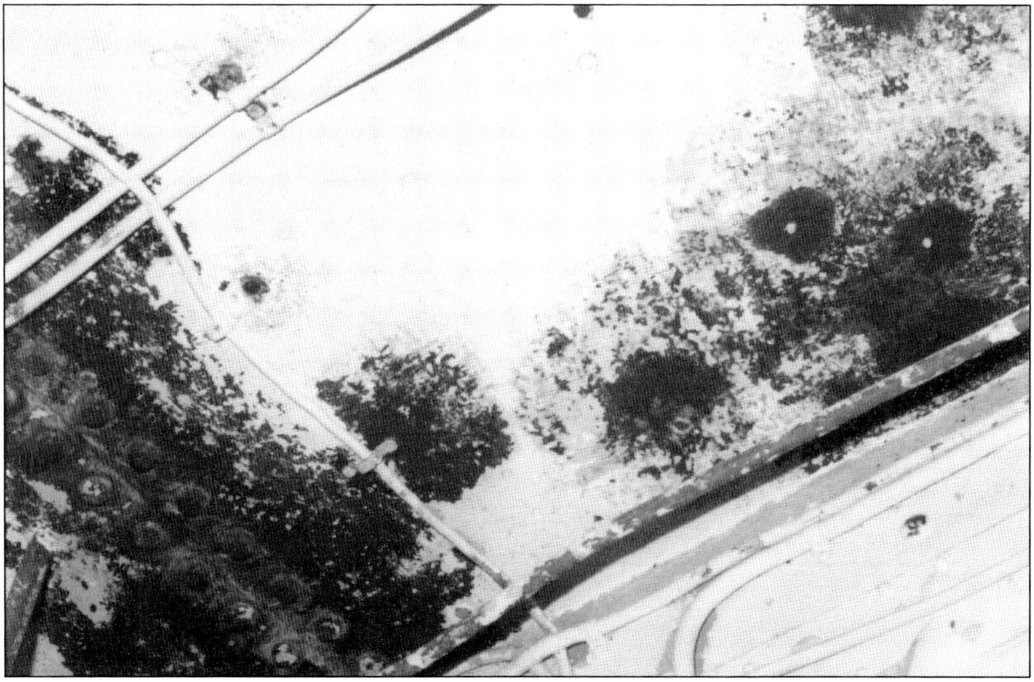

As a result, the decks had corroded so badly that holes had been eaten entirely through the steel underlayer. The holes could be seen clearly on the overhead of the compartments below the upper deck. Like a sponge, the rust retained water, accelerating the damage. (PC.)

Texas leaked so badly many compartments collected standing water, promoting rust and still more leaks, which allowed additional water to collect. It was a vicious cycle that would destroy the old ship within a decade if not arrested. (PC.)

A statewide fundraising drive was held in 1948 to raise money to move the battleship to Texas. In 1986, this was repeated. Various fundraising efforts were started, including an aluminum can recycling campaign, where the cans collected were cashed in and the proceeds donated to the Battleship Texas Commission's restoration effort. (TPWD.)

San Jacinto Day in 1986 was the Texas sesquicentennial, marking the 150th anniversary of the Battle of San Jacinto, which gained Texas independence from Mexico. The San Jacinto celebrations aboard *Texas* were bigger than ever and drew large crowds, but *Texas* needed to be dry docked to survive. (PC.)

On December 31, 1988, *Texas* left her berth at the San Jacinto Battlefield Park for the first time since 1948. It took six large tugs to pull *Texas* clear of the mud. From there, *Texas* made a 56-mile trip under tow to Todd Shipyard in Galveston. (PC.)

Once at Todd Shipyard, *Texas* was placed in its floating dry dock. It was a near-run thing. A leak developed in the hull near the engine room. *Texas* filled with water faster than the pumps could clear, and by the time it reached the dry dock, *Texas* was almost too low to get in. (PC.)

The first order of business was an inspection of the hull. Both bow and stern showed evidence of years of neglect. (PC.)

Close examination of the hull revealed numerous places where corrosion had eaten holes through the hull plating, allowing muddy Houston Ship Channel water to enter. Had repairs been delayed much longer, *Texas* would have been unsalvageable. (PC.)

Plating corroded past restoration was removed while *Texas* was at Todd Shipyard. Where necessary, the frames were replaced or reinforced. In all, over one-sixth of the hull structure of *Texas* was replaced at Todd Shipyard. (PC.)

Out with the old and in with the new. New steel plating was installed on *Texas* where necessary. Also removed were the 1.1-inch quad mounts that had been on *Texas* since 1948. They were replaced with 40-mm Bofors quad mounts to restore *Texas* to her 1945 appearance. (PC.)

Once the structural work was completed, *Texas* was towed from Todd Shipyard to Green's Bayou (on the Houston Ship Channel), where the ship was repainted in the dark blue camouflage Measure 21 it sported during the Iwo Jima and Okinawa campaigns. (PC.)

While at Green's Bayou, concrete covering the weather decks, which had been broken up earlier, was replaced by wood decking. Three Green's Bayou workers inspect their work after a long shift. (PC.)

A final step taken at Green's Bayou was to attach clamps to *Texas*'s hull. These were used to attach *Texas* to a new mooring system installed at the San Jacinto Battlefield Park while *Texas* was being refitted. Four monopile mooring posts were emplaced. (PC.)

Finally, after a two-year refit, *Texas* was ready to return to her permanent mooring at the San Jacinto Battleship Park. To celebrate, many of those who contributed to the preservation of *Texas* were invited aboard to share the trip. A rejuvenated *Texas* was returning home. (PC.)

A celebration needs a band. To add to the festivities, a band played jazz music as guests boarded *Texas* and during the trip down the Houston Ship Channel. It was July 26, 1990, almost 19 months to the day since *Texas* left for Todd Shipyard. (PC.)

Soon the tugs were in place and moving *Texas* down the Houston Ship Channel. While many aboard had spent a lot of time on *Texas* while it was floating in her berth, being on a moving *Texas* was a new experience. (PC.)

When *Texas* arrived at her berth, the final step was to attach her to the steel collars ringing each monopile pier. The advantage of this mooring arrangement is it allows *Texas* to rise or drop with the water level, even hurricane storm surges, remaining in place without adjusting mooring lines. (PC.)

There was still work to be done, so *Texas* did not reopen to the public until September 8, 1990. When it did finally open, a massive rededication ceremony was held. Large crowds attended the reopening. (PC.)

Among the visitors present at the reopening was a ship even older than *Texas*, the sailing barque *Elissa*. An iron-hulled cargo ship launched in 1877, *Elissa* is a museum ship in Galveston. It was sailed up from Galveston to join the festivities. (PC.)

Even before her refit, *Texas* was the site of many reunions of World War I veterans. Reunions of *Texas* crewmembers, such as this one in 1984, were regularly held at their old ship. By 1984, most surviving crew were in their late 50s to early 70s. (TPWD.)

Navy veterans were not the only ones meeting at the *Texas*. In 1992, a reunion of First Marine Division veterans was held aboard *Texas*. In World War II, *Texas* provided fire support for the First Marine Division at Okinawa. The reunion opened with a Marine color guard. (TPWD.)

When First Marine veterans boarded *Texas*, they were saluted by TPWD staff. The First Marine Division fought in every conflict from World War II to Desert Storm. Retired veterans from all eras attended. (TPWD.)

Another group that held a reunion at *Texas* was the surviving crew of the battleship *Oklahoma*. The reunion was held in 1995, when the youngest surviving veteran of *Oklahoma*, sunk at Pearl Harbor, would have been 71. Pipers played a lament for those killed at Pearl Harbor. (TPWD.)

Texas reached another landmark in 1998, marking her 50th year at the San Jacinto Battlefield and a half-century as a museum ship and war memorial. TPWD celebrated with two days of special events. (TPWD.)

Volunteers help out with *Texas*. A lot of work is done by the First Texas Volunteers who are out at *Texas* every weekend working on preservation and restoration. Other groups also help. This is a group of Boy Scouts from a local troop swabbing the forecastle deck. (AC.)

Docents are another set of volunteers helping *Texas*. They tell the history of the ship to visitors. This docent is telling some Scouts about *Texas* before they set to work cleaning the ship. (AC.)

The TPWD has expanded activities aboard *Texas* since her 1988–1990 refit. Included are Hard Hat Tours, which allow visitors access to parts of the ship normally closed to the general public. This group is inside one of the 14-inch gun turrets. (AC.)

Hard Hat Tours not only allow access to interesting parts of the ship, they are also a great way to learn about *Texas* as well. Volunteers restoring different parts of *Texas* tell Hard Hat participants about the different compartments. Here, a docent is explaining how *Texas*'s boilers work. (AC.)

Texas achieved another milestone in 2012, the centennial of her launching. Of the 63 dreadnoughts afloat when she was launched, only *Texas* remains. TPWD decided to celebrate the occasion in style. (GM.)

In addition to the speeches, a salute was fired from *Texas* to celebrate her 100th anniversary. The salute was fired by reenactors dressed as soldiers of the Texian Army, which won Texas independence from Mexico in 1836, and fired using a cannon replicating artillery of the Texas War of Independence. (GM.)

The salute was returned by Houston Port Authority tugboats using water cannons shooting sprays of red- and blue-colored water. (GM.)

While *Texas* has fought the ravages of time for over a century, today it has an ally in that fight: the dedicated staff of professionals who perform constant maintenance. This includes tasks such as constantly renewing the exposed wooden deck. (WL.)

What does the future hold for *Texas*? Plans call for her to be placed in a dry berth, similar to the one shown here. This should reduce hull corrosion caused by constant immersion in water and simplify maintenance. A dry berth will help ensure *Texas* survives another century. (TPWD.)

Three

THE *TEXAS* TODAY

Texas is already into its second century of existence. So what is it like today? Much of the ship is open to the public. For safety reasons, other parts of the *Texas* are closed to the public (and even the volunteers and staff) while other areas can be visited only with TPWD staff or volunteers present in special tours, such as the Hard Hat Tours.

This chapter presents a photographic tour of *Texas*, offering views of the public parts of the ship, compartments available on special tours, and even a few spots not normally accessible to the public.

The pictures are arranged to mimic an actual tour of *Texas*. It starts at the ramp where *Texas* is boarded. From there it makes a circuit of *Texas*'s first deck, the level at which *Texas* is entered. Starting at the ship's bell, it goes forward along the starboard side, up the superstructure to the navigation bridge, then back down to the first deck. Going forward along the starboard side to the bow, it then goes back along the port side, with stops in a main turret and the various first deck compartments.

From there, it descends to the second deck on the port side. On the second deck, it goes forward along the port side to the bow, back along the starboard side to the stern, and forward from the stern on the port side to roughly where the second deck tour started.

A circuit of the third deck follows, with descents into several working spaces, including the engine room, the boiler room, the communications center, the dynamo rooms, and the magazines and handling rooms for the 14-inch guns. Most of these areas are not open to the public.

Confused? A map of the ship is included on the next page to allow the images to be correlated with their location on the ship. This chapter can be used as a guide on an actual tour of the ship, or for a Walter Mitty–style armchair tour of *Texas*. Enjoy.

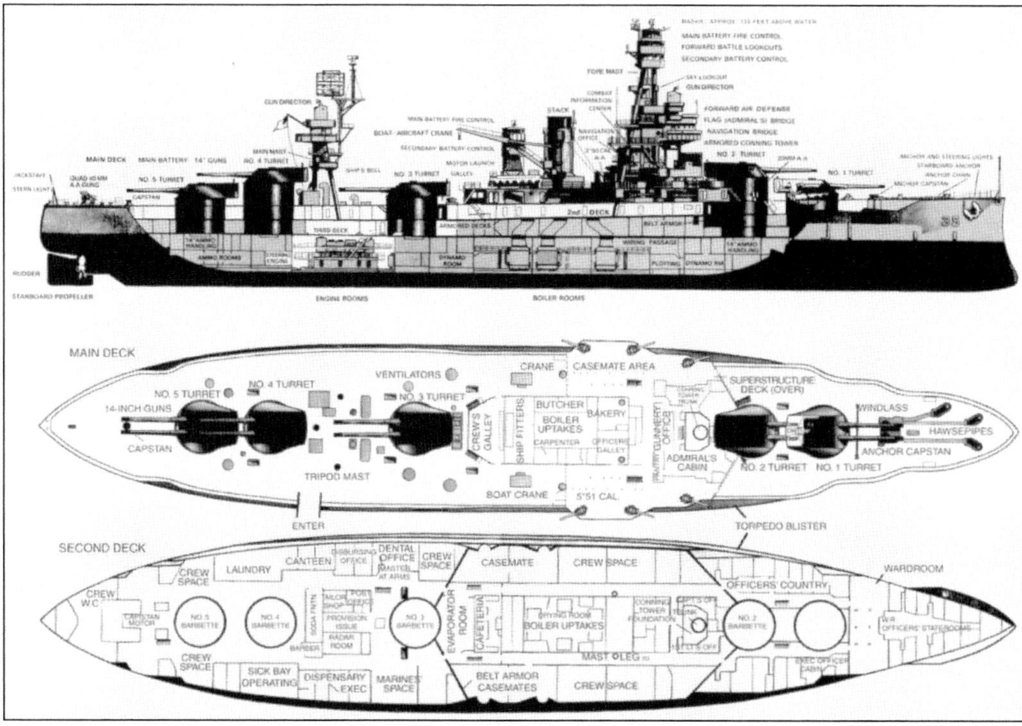

Pictured are plans of *Texas* showing the locations of points of interest. This virtual tour looks at objects on the weather decks (main deck and higher), then goes through the second deck, descends into the third deck, and finally examines working spaces normally inaccessible to the public. Reference this diagram to follow progress. (TPWD.)

To reach *Texas*, visitors travel an access road where they pass this propeller. It is one of the two propellers once used to drive *Texas* when she was in service. Removed when *Texas* became a museum ship, for many years it sat on the quarterdeck before being relocated here following the 1988–1990 refit. (WL.)

Texas is shown as she appears today. During the 1988–1990 refit, the ship was restored to her appearance in 1945. The 40-mm antiaircraft guns she had then were replaced, and she was repainted in a dark blue Measure 21 camouflage scheme. Over 25 years have passed since the refit, and constant maintenance is required. (WL.)

The ship's bell is attached to the back leg of the after tripod mast, between Turret 3 and Turret 4. It was used to mark the watches aboard ship. Reach it by going to the centerline of *Texas* after boarding from the gangway. (WL.)

Moving forward from the boarding gangway on the starboard (right) side of the main deck, one of the first objects passed is a three-inch antiaircraft gun. In 1945, *Texas* had 10 of these single-mount guns. Most were originally installed during the 1925 refit. At that time, they were cutting-edge. By 1945, they were obsolete. (WL.)

Ahead of the three-inch gun is one of the quad Bofors 40-mm antiaircraft mounts. In 1945, *Texas* had 10 quad 40-mm mounts, which were then state of the art. When *Texas* became a museum ship, the Navy replaced these with quad 1.1-inch mounts because the quad 40-mm was still being used. Replaced when *Texas* was refitted in 1989, these guns were originally mounted on *Iowa*-class ships. (WL.)

Amidships on the main deck is an area known as the "air castle." It contains the six remaining five-inch low-angle guns. *Texas* was built with 21 five-inch guns. Nineteen were mounted in casemates on the second deck, with two on the superstructure deck above the main deck. (WL.)

The air castle contains several of these boxes. These are ammunition hoists for the five-inch shells. During combat, they are normally closed, except when shells are being removed, to protect the magazines containing the shells. Several hoists on the air castle are open to show the interior. (WL.)

These hooks, attached to the beams on the air castle overhead, are hammock hooks. While *Texas* had bunks by 1945, the crew slept in hammocks when the ship was first launched. Even during World War II, *Texas* could not hold enough bunks to sleep every member of her crew, so some still slept in hammocks, even in the exposed air castle. (WL.)

This room served as the officer's galley when *Texas* was a Navy warship. Today it is the theater, where visitors can watch a video about *Texas*'s history. This room also contains the dud 240-mm shell that struck *Texas* at Cherbourg and the knot board from its naval days. There is also a larger-than-life-sized enlargement of the photograph on page 47. (WL.)

Forward of the officer's galley, one deck up on the superstructure deck, is the captain's cabin. It consisted of several rooms, including a sleeping area, bathroom, office area, and dining room (shown here). Jack McKeon lived in these quarters between 1949 and 1970. (WL.)

Two levels above the captain's cabin is the signal bridge. Among other items on it are searchlights, one of which is shown here. During World War I, searchlights were used to illuminate enemy targets at night. By World War II, radar replaced searchlights for nighttime surveillance, although searchlights were still used for signaling. (WL.)

At the aft end of this platform is a compass. Why is a compass there? There are a few different reasons. It allows the officer of the deck to watch the compass direction when backing. It also serves as a backup compass if the compass in the pilot house gets destroyed. (WL.)

From this position, the ship's steam whistle at the top of the smokestack can be seen. A steam line running from the boilers at the bottom of the stack straight up the smokestack provided access to boiler-generated steam. When *Texas* had two smokestacks, the whistle was on the forward stack. (WL.)

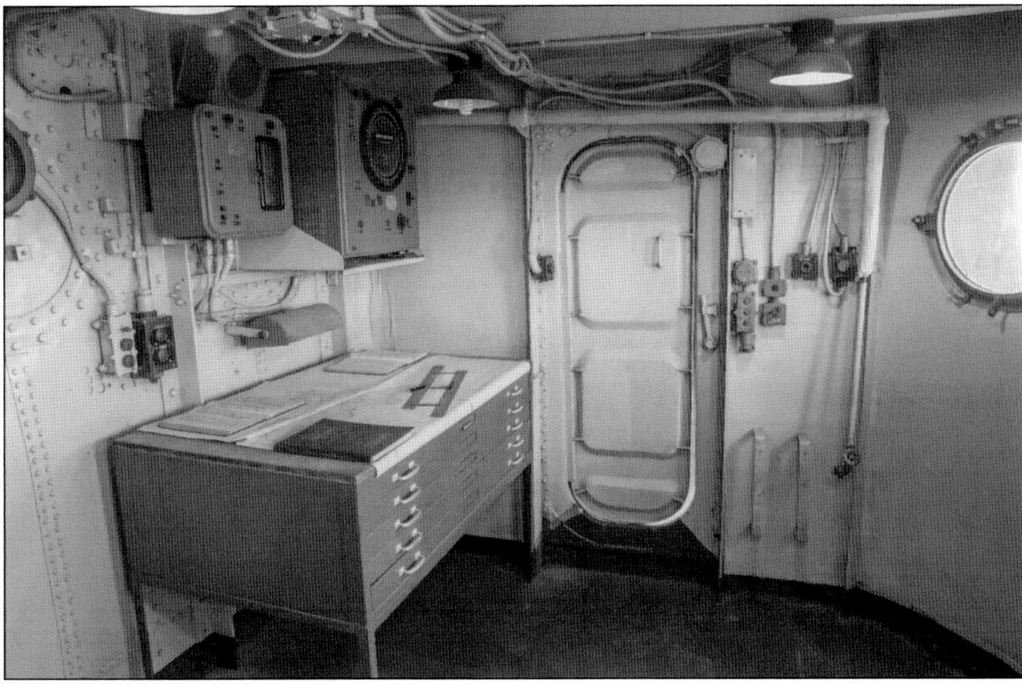

Above the signal bridge is the navigation bridge. *Texas* was navigated and steered on this level. At the back of the signal bridge is the chart house. Navigation maps were stored in the map cabinet, and much of the navigation was done here. (WL.)

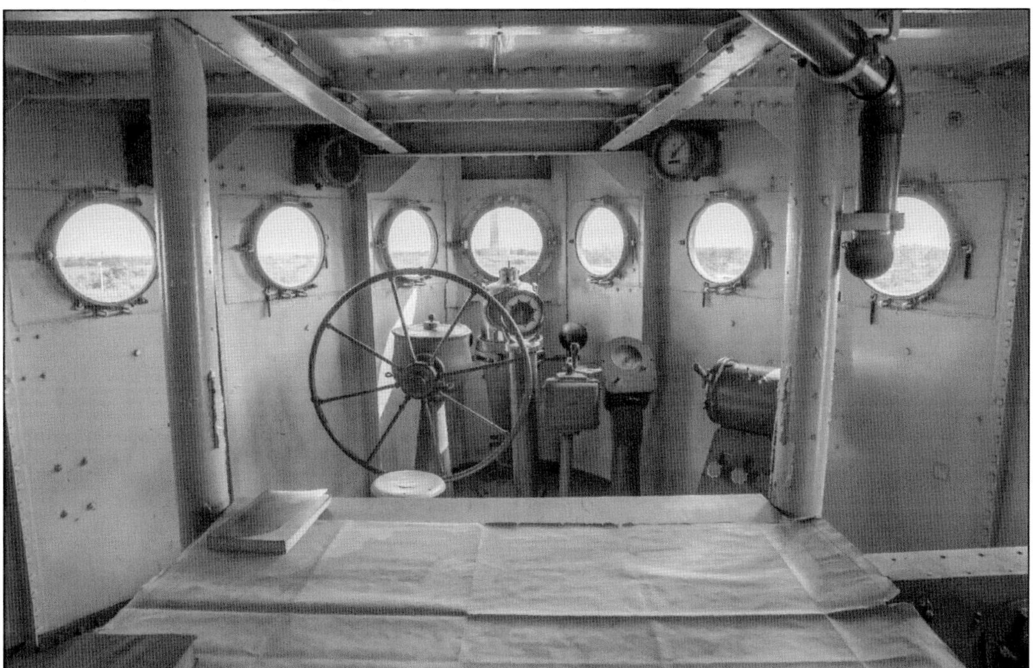

Ahead of the chart house, separated by a bridge radio room and the captain's sea cabin, is the pilot house. The ship was steered from here. It contains the ship's wheel, a magnetic compass, a gyro compass, the engine telegraph (to command the engine speed), and a radar scope. (WL.)

Returning to the main deck level and moving forward of the air castle brings visitors to two of the Oerlikon 20-mm antiaircraft guns carried by *Texas*. These were short-range guns, useful only within 3,000 yards. In 1945, *Texas* carried 44 of these guns. (WL.)

Forward of these 20-mm guns are Turrets 1 and 2. Each turret has two 14-inch guns, capable of firing a 1,400-pound shell up to 18 nautical miles. Forward of Turret 1 is the windlass, used to move mooring or tow lines. (WL.)

Forward of the turrets is *Texas*'s forecastle. It contains the ship's ground tackle, the chains that hold the ship's anchors, and the capstans that raise and lower the anchor chains. The capstans are the squat barrel-shaped cylinders the chain is wrapped around. (WL.)

The view from inside Turret 1 shows the left gun. The breech is open. One of the powder bags containing propellant is on the tray. The propellant, standard propellant formulation, or SDP, was a mixture of nitrocellulose and diphenylamine. Four propellant bags were used to fire a 14-inch shell. (WL.)

On the port side of Turret 2's barbette, a paravane is mounted. In wartime, *Texas* would have carried at least two, one on each side of the turret. Paravanes were used to sweep mines. When would a battleship be used as a minesweeper? Only when absolutely no other option existed. (WL.)

Moving aft along the port side of the superstructure takes visitors to three compartments dear to any sailor's heart. The first is the bakery. Bread, pies, and cobblers were prepared here. Some paint is peeling, but the ovens and mixers are still there. (WL.)

Aft of the bakery is the butcher shop. When *Texas* was in service, most of the crew aboard were meat and potato men. Beef and pork were cut up here for use by the ship's cooks. (WL.)

Immediately aft of the butcher was the shipfitters' shop. Behind that was the crew's galley. It was located on the main deck rather than below so cooking odors and smoke would not be trapped below. Food was sent to the cafeteria, on the second deck, using a dumbwaiter. (WL.)

Moving forward down the port air castle ladder to the second deck brings visitors to this armored door. *Texas* used casemate armor, where the center of the ship was heavily protected, but the ends were only lightly armored. This armored door, at the end of the casemate, shows how thick the main armor belt was. (WL.)

There are lots of little details on *Texas* that are easy to miss. This is a battle lamp mounted on the bulkhead in officer's country, where the officers' cabins were located on the second deck forward of the casemate. It could be used for emergency lighting if power failed. (WL.)

In the middle of officers' country is the wardroom. It spans the width of the ship and serves as a combination dining room, recreation room, and club for *Texas*'s officers. This dining table shows the type of china and the chairs the officers used. (WL.)

The silver service given to *Texas* in 1914 is still aboard a century later. It is displayed in the wardroom, where it would have been kept during *Texas*'s naval career. It would have been used on formal occasions. Since *Texas* served as a flagship, formal occasions happened frequently. (WL.)

The wardroom also served as the trophy room, where any sports or battle trophies won by *Texas* would have been displayed. In addition to the sports trophies in this case, the wardroom still contains the silver model of *De Zeven Provincien* presented to *Texas* by the Holland-American Line. (WL.)

The wardroom also contains the builder's plate for *Texas*. She was the 147th hull built at Newport News Shipbuilding and Dry Dock Company. Although *Texas* was launched in 1912, she was not completed until 1913. (WL.)

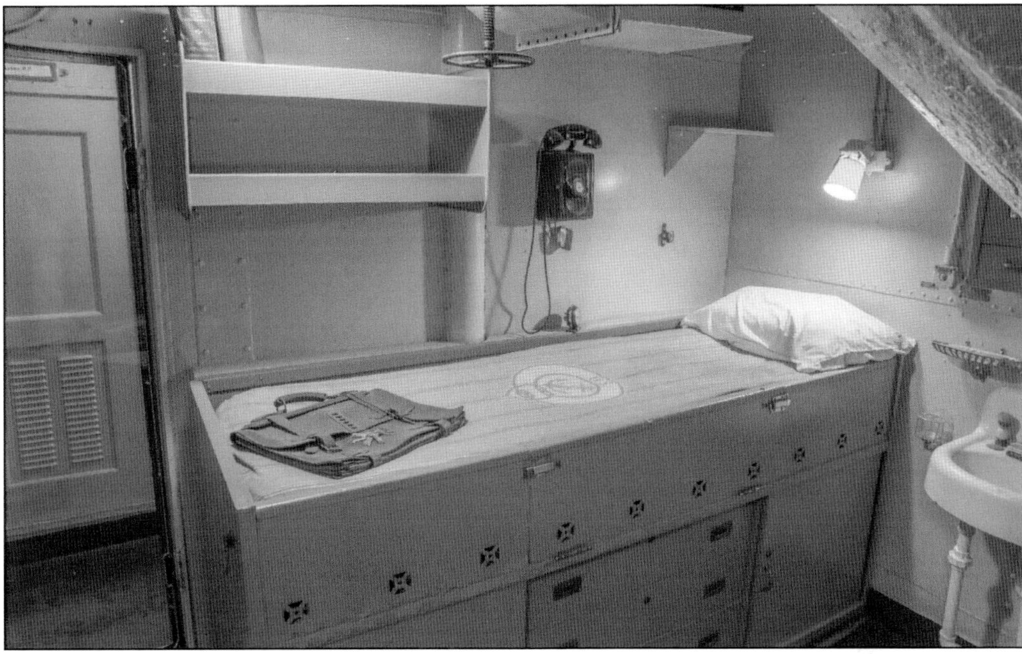

One of the officer staterooms near the wardroom is shown here. During World War II, *Texas*'s surgeon slept here. The picture shows the amenities an officer could expect—his own sink, a bunk with storage drawers, and a bookshelf. On the opposite wall is a desk. Note the battle phone above the bunk. (WL.)

Aft of the wardroom between the barbettes for Turrets 1 and 2 was the officers' pantry. Mess stewards would prepare the plates for meals in this pantry and clean the dishes and silver afterwards. (WL.)

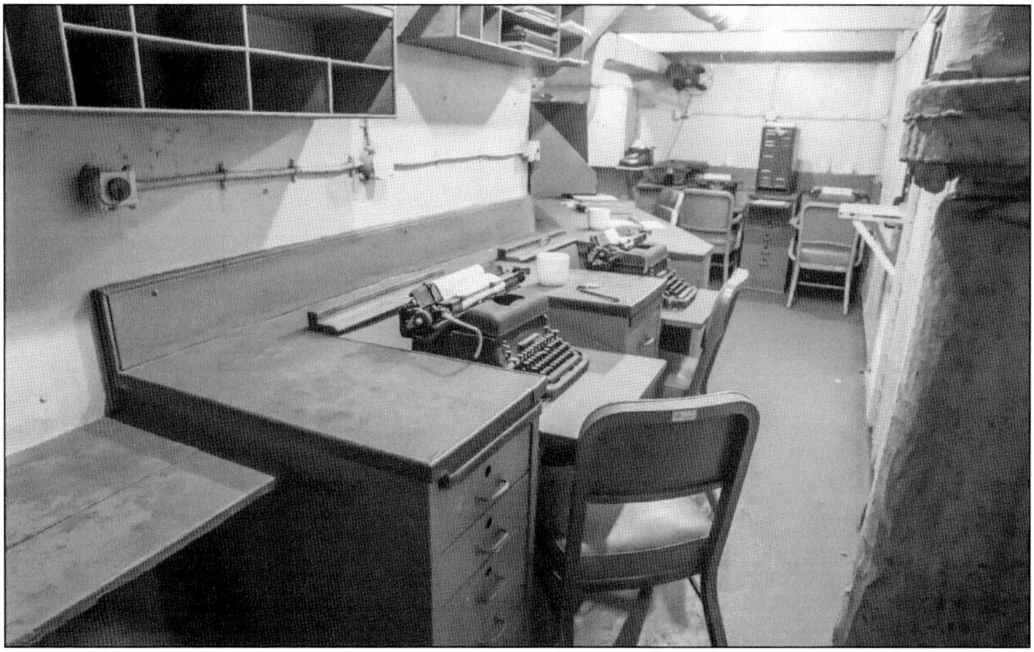

Just aft of the Turret 1 barbette on the second deck, under the bridge, are the ship's offices. On the port side is the captain's office. The starboard side has the first lieutenant's office, shown here. Much of the day-to-day maintenance of the ship's material condition was managed at this office. (WL.)

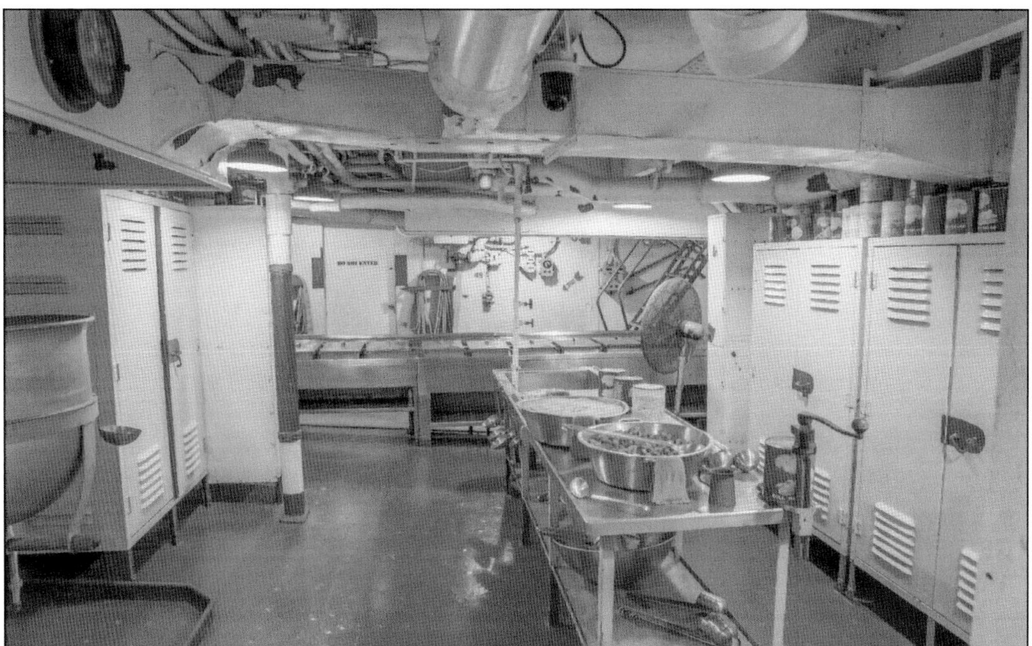

The cafeteria, shown here, was immediately below the kitchen. After it was added, sailors got their own meals here, rather than having another sailor serving as messman for a mess of 8–12 sailors. He then took it to the crew space where the mess lived and ate. (WL.)

Just aft of the casemate, on the starboard side, was the Marine Space, where *Texas*'s marine contingent lived. The marine space contained the light arms armory, the rifles used by the Marines. The sewing machine was used to keep Marine uniforms just so. (WL.)

The Marines served as guards aboard the ship and could also be used to provide troops for landing parties. They lived next to their armory, with their uniform and gear in lockers next to their bunks. (WL.)

The Marine sergeant had a cabin in the Marine Space. Tucked at the front of the Marine Space, it served as a combination sleeping quarters and office for "Gunny." (WL.)

The Exec Office is aft of the Marine Space. This office focused on personnel assignment and management of the enlisted members of *Texas*. Battleships floated on paperwork. (WL.)

Aft of the Exec Office, on the same side of the corridor, is the dispensary. This served as the pharmacy for *Texas*. Medicines of all types were stored here. The dispensary could prepare whatever the doctor ordered for a member of the crew. (WL.)

Across the corridor from the dispensary was the Auxiliary Combat Information Center, located beyond the door. In combat, *Texas*'s guns were directed from the main Combat Information Center (CIC) below the signal bridge. The Auxiliary CIC served as backup if the main CIC was knocked out. Both contained communications equipment, plotting boards, radar displays, and information needed to manage combat operations. (WL.)

Aft of the Auxiliary CIC was the barbershop. Open six and a half hours per day when *Texas* was in commission, today it stands empty, its three chairs waiting for sailors who left for good 70 years ago. (WL.)

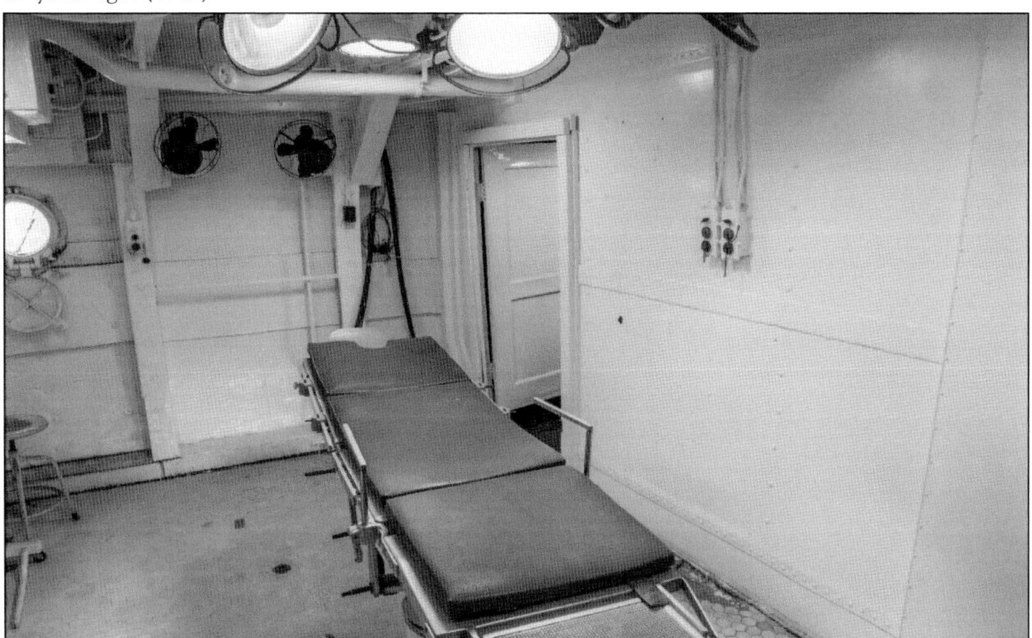
Back on the outboard side of the corridor, separated from the dispensary by the doctor's office, is *Texas*'s surgical theater. It could tend to the needs of combat injuries or shipboard accidents. Except for those injured when Cherbourg was bombarded, most of the combat casualties treated here came from outside the battleship. (WL.)

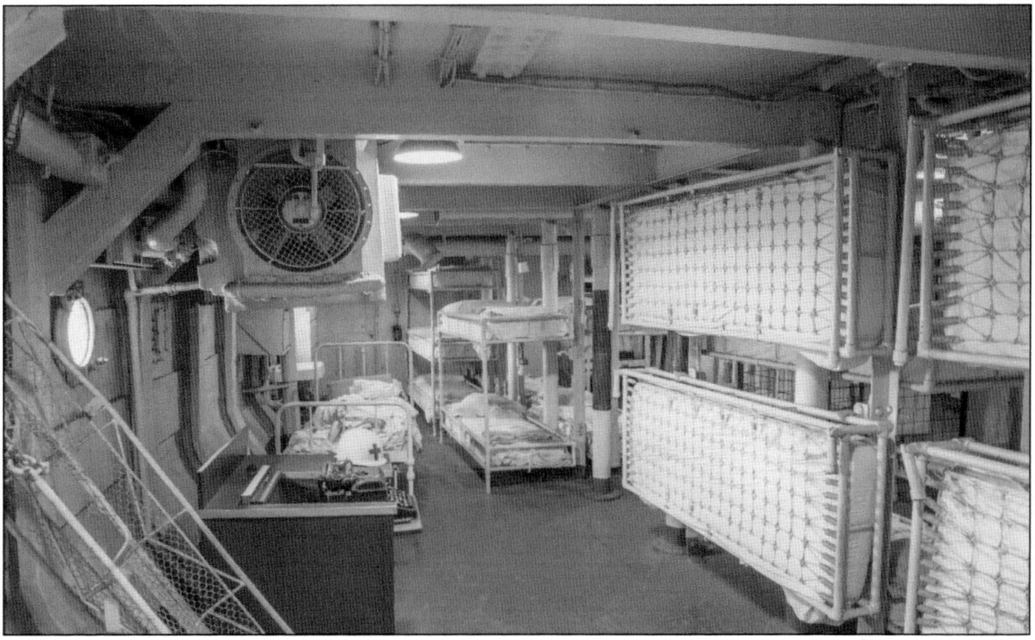

Just aft of the surgery was sick bay. Sailors, or anyone brought aboard, sufficiently injured or ill enough to require nursing care were kept in the sick bay. A Stokes basket, similar to those used to transfer casualties to and from *Texas*, can be seen in the foreground. (WL.)

Aft of the medical facilities, between the Turret 5 barbette and crew washrooms, is a clipping room for 20-mm ammunition. It was ready reserve storage for the cylindrical clips of 20-mm ammunition *Texas* used for antiaircraft defense. (WL.)

Near the stern on the second deck are the crew facilities. This is the washroom. The rectangular area on the deck on the left side of the picture shows the showers. The raised troughs are sinks. Through the door the toilets can be seen. Privacy was minimal. (WL.)

At the stern on the second deck is a clipping room for 40-mm ammunition. As with the 20-mm clipping room, this is not a magazine as much as ready-reserve storage for 40-mm ammunition. The 40-mm Borfors were *Texas*'s primary antiaircraft protection. (WL.)

Moving forward from the washroom on the port side brings visitors past one of the many crew spaces. This is typical of living arrangements for enlisted crew. Bunks were racks four-high, which folded up during the daytime. The table is where a mess of up to 14 men would eat. (WL.)

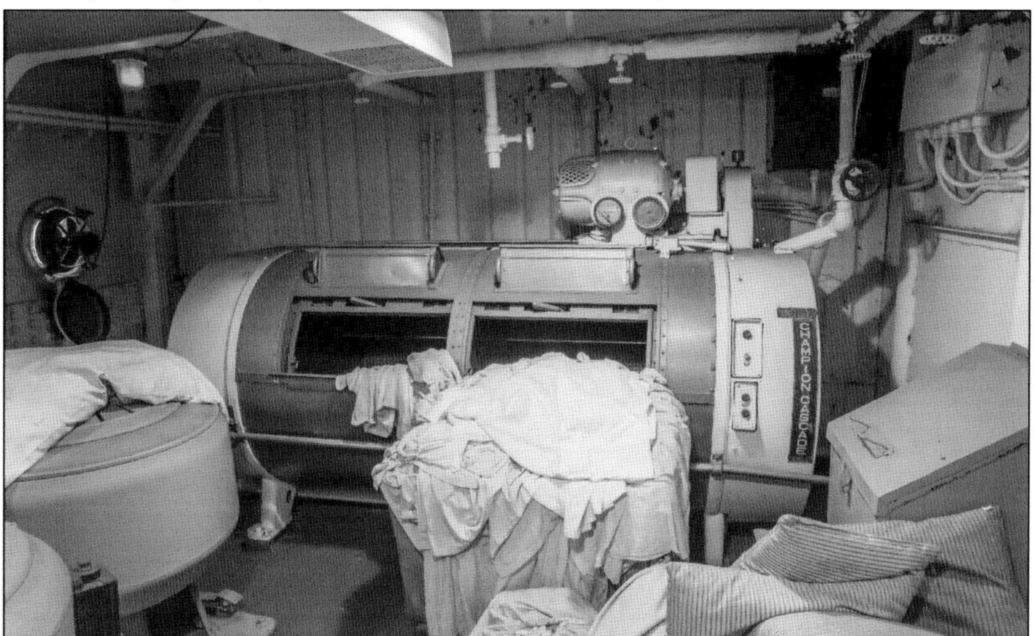

The second deck, port side corridor between Turret 5 and Turret 3 was *Texas*'s "Main Street." Aftermost, on the outboard side, was the ship's laundry. It has been restored to its 1945 appearance. The laundry was used to clean both clothing and bedding used by *Texas*'s crew of 1,600-plus men. (WL.)

Forward of the laundry is the canteen—the seagoing equivalent of a convenience store. Here, sailors could buy all manner of things, including cigarettes and tobacco products, "pogey-bait" (candy), magazines, soap, shoeshine supplies, shaving gear, and other marvelous stuff. (WL.)

Across the corridor from the canteen was another high point for sailors aboard *Texas*, especially the younger ones—the soda fountain. Just like the one at the Main Street five-and-dime of the 1940s, the soda fountain served Coca-Cola, soft-serve ice cream, and all manner of sundaes to suit a teenaged seaman's sweet tooth. (WL.)

Forward of the soda fountain was *Texas*'s tailor's shop. Uniforms could be altered or clothing repaired, just like at a period haberdashery. Since sailors had to pay for alterations, most enlisted men did their own tailoring, and the tailor shop was patronized mainly by commissioned or senior warrant officers. (WL.)

Next to the tailor's shop was a place used by the entire crew, the ship's post office. Mail was handled here, incoming and outgoing. Sailors could send money orders or registered mail, hence the safe. One testimony to how crowded *Texas* was? There were bunks in the post office where its staff slept. (WL.)

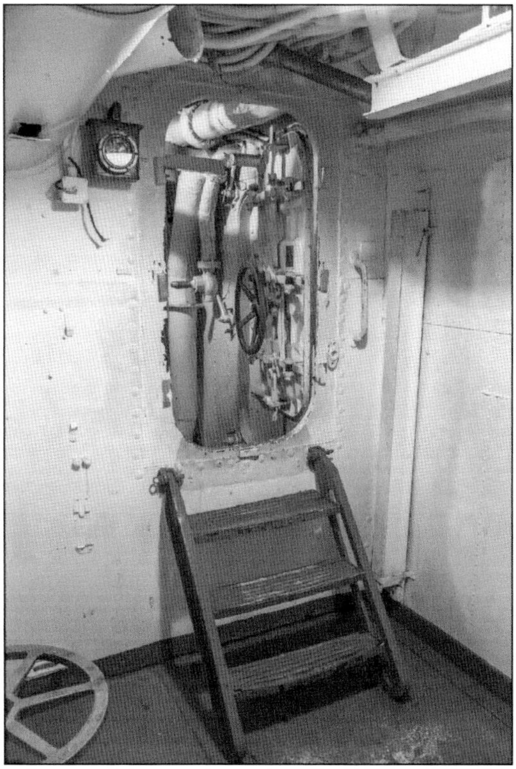

Finishing the tour of the second deck, visitors descend to the third deck, the lowest one accessible to the general public. Since the third deck is below the waterline, doorways are two feet above the deck, to contain flooding in case of damage. (WL.)

Damage control, stores storage, and ammunition handling are done on the third deck. This is the ammunition passageway. The rail overhead is used to move 14-inch shells from one end of the ship to the other. Above the rail are stored shoring timbers used to reinforce damaged bulkheads. These may have been here since *Texas* was commissioned. (WL.)

The third deck also has five-inch ammo hoists to carry five-inch shells from their magazines to the third deck. The shells, which weighed between 50 and 55 pounds, were then carried to a second hoist to take them to the air castle. The separation protected the magazine. (WL.)

Even the third deck, crowded with machinery, workshops, and store rooms, served as home for part of *Texas*'s crew. This is a crew space on the third deck, near the Turret 3 barbette. Note the 14-inch transfer rail arcing around the barbette. (WL.)

Damage control is managed from the third deck. This compartment is the damage control locker. It contains tools and equipment for making emergency repairs. The cones on the shelf are wooden plugs for plugging shot holes. Wrenches, fire axes, and sleeves for patching leaking pipes are also present. (WL.)

The third deck also contained the ship's brig. There are five cells in *Texas*'s brig. Each cell contains four steel walls, a steel deck, and a thin mattress by way of amenities. Misbehavior was not worth it. (WL.)

Working spaces are reached from the third deck. This is the passageway to the engine room, which contains two triple-expansion steam engines that drive *Texas*. The engine room is normally accessible to the general public. The engine rooms were closed from 2007 to 2010 for restoration and closed again for repairs between 2012 and 2014. (WL.)

The starboard triple-expansion steam engine is pictured here. Each engine has four cylinders: one high pressure, one medium pressure, and two low pressure. The engines are large. The high pressure cylinder has a 39-inch diameter, while the low pressure cylinders were 83 inches in diameter. All cylinders had a 48-inch stroke. (WL.)

The ship's engineers monitored the steam pressure entering and exiting each cylinder from this panel. Steam enters the high-pressure cylinder, is exhausted to the medium pressure cylinder, and then to the low pressure cylinders. Each cylinder is larger than the previous one, starting at the exit pressure of the previous cylinder. (WL.)

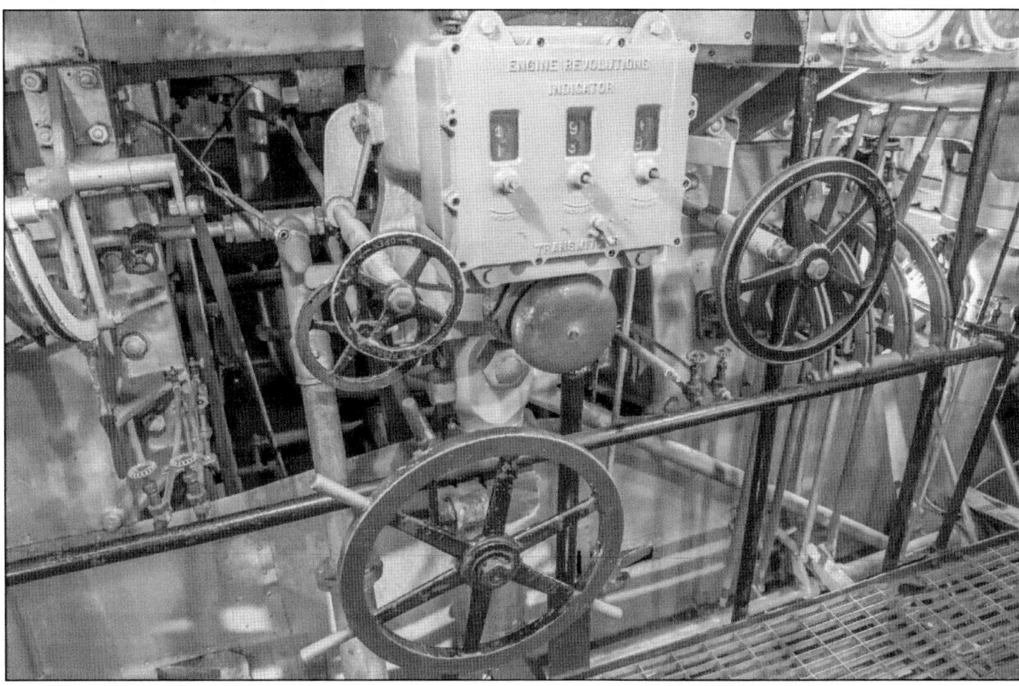

These valves regulate steam going into the cylinders. The box with the numbers is the engine revolutions indicator. It monitors the speed at which the engines turn the propeller shaft. *Texas* has a direct drive with no gearbox. The propeller turns at the same speed as the engine. (WL.)

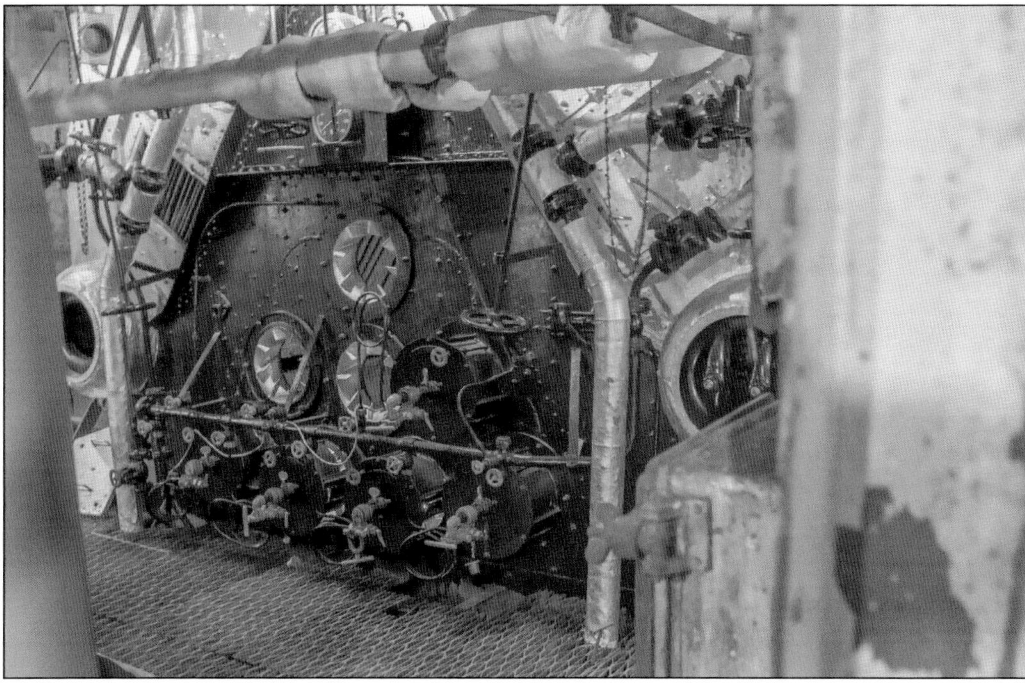

Steam to drive the engines is generated by the six Bureau Express oil-fired boilers. The one shown here has been restored by *Texas* volunteers. These boilers replaced the original 14 coal-fired boilers. The boiler room is not open to the general public, but is visited on the Hard Hat Tour. (WL.)

This is the combustion chamber of a Bureau Express boiler aboard *Texas*. The pipes at the top of the chamber are water-filled. Heat from the burning fuel oil superheats the water to steam at 265 pounds per square inch. The steam is then fed to the engines. (WL.)

The engineer of the watch oversaw the operation of *Texas*'s boilers and steam engine from this desk. It has not been restored and awaits future attention by volunteer workers. (WL.)

Also reached from the third deck are the radio and coding rooms and the plotting room. This ladder admits people to the plotting room, near the bottom of *Texas*. Since the plotting room was used to aim *Texas*'s guns, it was placed in a location where enemy gunfire was least likely to damage it. (WL.)

Compartments in lower levels of *Texas* were reached through small, watertight doors. They were kept small so they could be easily sealed if one compartment started flooding. The small size slowed passage through these doors, and sailors manning these compartments could easily get trapped in them by battle damage. (WL.)

Pictured is one of the plotting boards in the plotting room, where a team tracked potential targets for *Texas*'s guns and determined the solution for hitting the target. This solution provided the angles for orientation of the turret and the elevation of the guns in the turret. (AC.)

The main radio room of *Texas* is also on the third deck. Radio communications with the outside world went through this room. The radio room has been partly restored by volunteers. Local hams have also restored the vacuum-tube radios used aboard *Texas*. Finding working radio tubes is challenging. (WL.)

Coded messages would be passed through the open hatch to the decoding room. There, classified signals would be decoded and the resulting message passed to the captain on the bridge using pneumatic tubes. A Marine guard stood outside the decoding room to preserve its secrets. (WL.)

A battleship built in 1912 was not ADA or OSHA compliant. This passageway leads to the dynamo room, deep within the *Texas*. This area is not accessible to the general public and only accessible to TPWD staff with difficulty. It illustrates the challenges of keeping *Texas* in shape. (WL.)

This dynamo generated electricity for *Texas*. The steam-powered dynamos provided the electricity needed to operate the battleship. *Texas* had two dynamo rooms with two dynamos each. Each dynamo produced 400,000 watts for a total of 1.6 megawatts of power. This dynamo is in the forward dynamo room. (WL.)

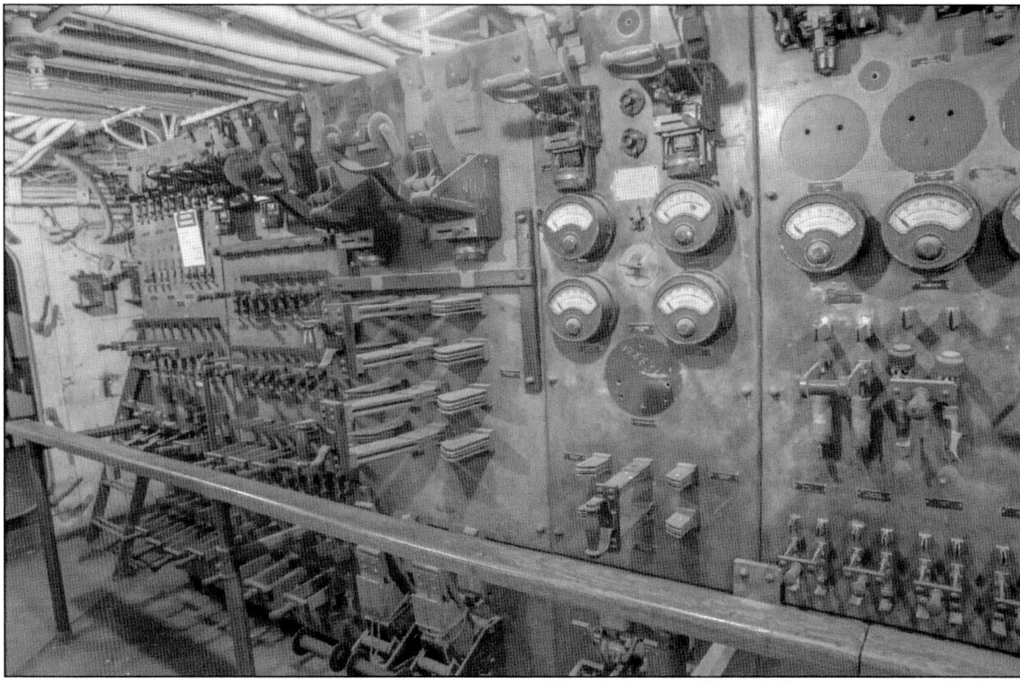

Power generated by the dynamos was distributed to where it was needed using this distribution board. *Texas* used 125-volt, direct current electricity for most electrical functions. This power distribution board is also in the forward dynamo room, two levels below the third deck. (WL.)

Texas's main battery of 14-inch guns was the reason for her existence. To feed these guns, deep within the depth of *Texas*, are rooms containing the gun's shells and propellant. This is a forward 14-inch shell magazine. It is located on the first platform, two levels below the third deck. Each turret has two such magazines, one on each side of it. (WL.)

Four cylindrical bags of guncotton propelled the shells. The bags were stored in powder rooms on the first platform located between Turrets 1 and 2 and 4 and 5 and in front of Turret 3. For safety, each bag, which weighed nearly 100 pounds, was kept in a metal container until ready for use. (WL.)

Shell and powder went to the shell-handling room, located at the base of each turret, when they were needed and sent to the turret using the hoist shown here. The shell was sent up first. Powder bags reached the handling room through the drums at the back of the photograph to isolate the explosive from the turret. (WL.)

More 14-inch shells were also stored in the base of the Turrets 2 and 4 barbettes. The shells were stored nose-down on *Texas*. Two ranks of shells ringed the edge of each barbette. (WL.)

The barbette for Turret 2 stored more than just the 14-inch shells. When *Texas* was in service, the three shelves in this photograph held the contents of the midshipmen's library. Why here? The barbette was climate controlled, and the midshipmen bunked just ahead of the barbette on this level of the battleship. (WL.)

Bibliography

BB35 Booklet of General Plans. Puget Sound Naval Yard, WA: United States Navy, 1944.

Ferguson, John C. *Historic Battleship Texas: The Last Dreadnought* (Military History of Texas Series). Austin, TX: State House Press, 2007.

"Institutional History, Battleship Texas BB35." La Porte, TX: Texas Parks and Wildlife Department internal document, 2016.

Power, Hugh. *Battleship Texas* (Centennial Series of the Association of Former Students, Texas A&M University). College Station, TX: Texas A&M University Press, 1993.

San Jacinto Battleground/Battleship Texas. Texas Parks and Wildlife. www.facebook.com, accessed January 18, 2016.

"Texas II (Battleship No. 35)." Naval History and Heritage Command. www.history.navy.mil/research/histories/ship-histories/danfs/t/texas-ii.html, accessed January 18, 2016.

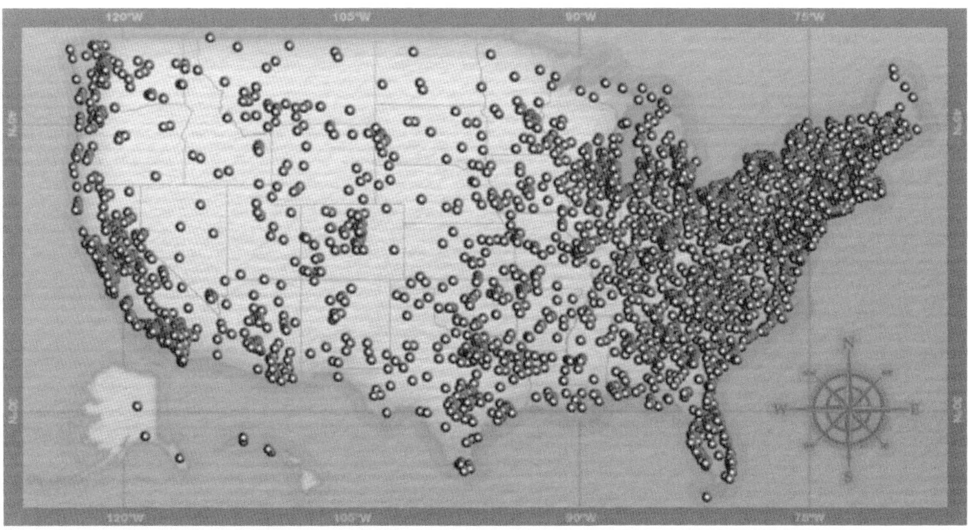